Mental Toughness

Nurturing Your Inner Resilience for Success

Swami Vivekananda

Institute of Thought & Philosophy

GRAPEVINE INDIA

Published by

GRAPEVINE INDIA PUBLISHERS PVT LTD

www.grapevineindia.com
Delhi | Mumbai
email: grapevineindiapublishers@gmail.com

Ordering Information:
Quantity sales: Special discounts are available on quantity purchases by corporations, associations, and others.
For details, reach out to the publisher.

First published by Grapevine India 2023

The mission of the Institute of Thought and Philosophy is to preserve and propagate the teachings of Swami Vivekananda. This great Indian spiritual leader is known for introducing the West to Hinduism. Drawing from his vast literary legacy, we provide valuable insights and practical guidance for modern living.

Have any query or feedback? Please reach out to us at ITPPress123@gmail.com

Attaining Perfection

My ideal indeed can be put into a few words and that is: to preach unto mankind their divinity, and how to make it manifest in every movement of life.

It is an obvious fact that, with the exception of what is taken up by the necessities of life, the man of culture is loath to spend his time on so-called comforts, and even necessary actions are performed with lessened zeal, as the process moves forward. Even luxuries are arranged according to ideas and ideals, to make them reflect as much of thought-life as possible.

True love never comes until the object of our love becomes to us our highest ideal. It may be that in many cases human love is misdirected and misplaced, but to the person who loves, the thing he loves is always his own highest idea. One may see his ideal in the vilest of beings, and another in the highest of beings; nevertheless, in every case it is the ideal alone that can be truly and intensely loved.

The highest ideal of every man is called God. Ignorant or wise, saint or sinner, man or woman, educated or uneducated, cultivated or uncultivated, to every human being the highest ideal is God. The synthesis of all the highest ideals of beauty, of sublimity, and of power gives us the completest conception of the loving and lovable God.

These ideals exist in some shape or other in every mind naturally; they form a part and parcel of all our minds. All the active manifestations of human nature are struggles of those ideals to become realised in practical life. All the various movements that we see around us in society are caused by the various ideals in various souls trying to come out and become concretised; what is inside presses on to come outside.

This perennially dominant influence of the ideal is the one force, the one motive power, that may be seen to be constantly working in the midst of mankind. It may be after hundreds of births, after struggling through thousands of years, that man finds that it is vain to try to make the inner ideal mould completely the external conditions and square well with them; after realising this he no more tries to project his own ideal on the outside world, but worships the ideal itself as ideal from the highest standpoint of love.

This ideally perfect ideal embraces all lower ideals. Every one admits the truth of the saying that a lover sees Helen's beauty on an Ethiop's brow. The man who is standing aside as a looker-on sees that love is here misplaced, but the lover sees his Helen all the same and does not see the Ethiop at all. Helen or Ethiop, the objects of our love are really the centres round which our ideals become crystallised.

What is it that the world commonly worships? Not certainly this all-embracing, ideally perfect ideal of the supreme devotee and lover. That ideal which men and women commonly worship is what is in themselves; every person projects his or her own ideal on the outside world and kneels before it.

That is why we find that men who are cruel and blood-thirsty conceive of a bloodthirsty God, because they can only love their own highest ideal. That is why good men have a very high ideal of God, and their ideal is indeed so very different from that of others.

For the ordinary man and the beginner, steady devotion (Nishtha) to an ideal is of paramount importance.

It is a great thing to take up a grand ideal in life and then give up one's whole life to it. For what otherwise is the value of life, this vegetating, little, low life of man? Subordinating it to one high ideal is the only value that life has.

Everyone can see the sky, even the very worm crawling upon the earth sees the blue sky, but how very far away it is! So it is with our ideal. It is far away, no doubt, but at the same time, we know that we must have it. We must even have the highest ideal.

Unfortunately in this life, the vast majority of persons are groping through this dark life without any ideal at all. If a man with an ideal makes a thousand mistakes, I am sure that the man without an ideal makes fifty thousand.

Therefore, it is better to have an ideal. And this ideal we must hear about as much as we can, till it enters into our hearts, into our brains, into our very veins, until it tingles in every drop of our blood and permeates every pore in our body. We must meditate upon it. "Out of the fullness of the heart the mouth speaketh," and out of the fullness of the heart the hand works too.

It is knowledge that opens the door to regions of wonder, knowledge that makes a god of an animal: and that knowledge which brings us to That, "knowing which everything else is known" (the heart of all knowledge — whose pulsation brings life to all sciences — the science of religion) is certainly the highest, as it alone can make man live a complete and perfect life in thought. Blessed be the land which has styled it "supreme science"!

The principle is seldom found perfectly expressed in the practical, yet the ideal is never lost. On the one hand, it is our duty never to lose sight of the ideal, whether we can approach it with sensible steps, or crawl towards it with imperceptible motion: on the other hand, the truth is, it is always loosening in front of us — though we try our best to cover its light with our hands before our eyes.

The life of the practical is in the ideal. It is the ideal that has penetrated the whole of our lives, whether we philosophise, or perform the hard, everyday duties of life. The rays of the ideal, reflected and refracted in various straight or tortuous lines, are pouring in through every aperture and windhole, and consciously or unconsciously, every function has to be performed in its light, every object has to be seen transformed, heightened, or deformed by it.

It is the ideal that has made us what we are, and will make us what we are going to be. It is the power of the ideal that has enshrouded us, and is felt in our joys or sorrows, in our great acts or mean doings, in our virtues and vices.

If such is the power of the ideal over the practical, the practical is no less potent in forming the ideal. The truth of the ideal is in the practical. The fruition of the ideal has been through the sensing of the practical. That the ideal is there is a proof of the existence of the practical somehow, somewhere. The ideal may be vaster, yet it is the multiplication of little bits of the practical. The ideal mostly is the summed-up, generalized, practical units.

The power of the ideal is in the practical. Its work on us is in and through the practical. Through the practical, the ideal is brought down to our sense-perception, changed into a form fit for our assimilation. Of the practical we make the steps to rise to the ideal. On that we build our hopes; it gives us courage to work.

One man who manifests the ideal in his life is more powerful than legions whose words can paint it in the most beautiful colours and spin out the finest principles.

He who desires for a comfortable and nice life and at the same time wants to realise the Self is like the fool who, wanting to cross the river, caught hold of a crocodile mistaking it for a log of wood. "Seek ye first the Kingdom of God and His righteousness, and all these things shall be added unto you."

Unto him everything who does not care for anything. Fortune is like a flirt; she cares not for him who wants her, but she is at the feet of him who does not care for her. Money comes and showers itself upon one who does not care for it; so does fame come in abundance until it is a trouble and a burden.

They always come to the Master. The slave never gets anything. The Master is he who can live in spite of them, whose life does not depend upon the little, foolish things of the world. Live for an ideal, and that one ideal alone. Let it be so great, so strong, that there may be nothing else left in the mind; no place for anything else, no time for anything else.

That is the one great first step — the real desire for the ideal. Everything comes easy after that. It is not truth, but development, that is the great aim. The struggle is the great lesson. Mind you, the great benefit in this life is struggle. It is through that we pass.

If there is any road to Heaven, it is through Hell. Through Hell to Heaven is always the way. When the soul has wrestled with circumstance and has met death, a thousand times death on the way, but nothing daunted has struggled forward again and again and yet again — then the soul comes out as a giant and laughs at the ideal he has been struggling for, because he finds how much greater is he than the ideal.

I am the end, my own Self, and nothing else, for what is there to compare to me own Self? Can a bag of gold be the ideal of my Soul? Certainly not! My Soul is the highest ideal that I can have. Realising my own real nature is the one goal of my life.

The ideal man of our ancestors was the Brahmin. In all our books stands out prominently this ideal of the Brahmin.

In Europe there is my Lord the Cardinal, who is struggling hard and spending thousands of pounds to prove the nobility of his ancestors, and he will not be satisfied until he has traced his ancestry to some dreadful tyrant who lived on a hill and watched the people passing by, and whenever he had the opportunity, sprang out on them and robbed them. That was the business of these nobility-bestowing ancestors, and my Lord Cardinal is not satisfied until he can trace his ancestry to one of these.

In India, on the other hand, the greatest princes seek to trace their descent to some ancient sage who dressed in a bit of loin cloth, lived in a forest, eating roots and studying the Vedas. It is there that the Indian prince goes to trace his ancestry. You are of the high caste when you can trace your ancestry to a Rishi, and not otherwise.

Our ideal of high birth, therefore, is different from, that of others. Our ideal is the Brahmin of spiritual culture and renunciation. By the Brahmin ideal what do I mean? I mean the ideal Brahmin-ness in which worldliness is altogether absent and true wisdom is abundantly present. That is the ideal of the Hindu race.

The ideal of man is to see God in everything. But if you cannot see Him in everything, see Him in one thing, in that thing which you like best, and then see Him in another. So on you can go. There is infinite life before the soul. Take your time and you will achieve your end.

Without the supernatural sanction as it is called, or the perception of the superconscious as I prefer to term it, there can be no ethics. Without the struggle towards the Infinite there can be no ideal. Any system that wants to bind men down to the limits of their own societies is not able to find an explanation for the ethical laws of mankind.

The Utilitarian wants us to give up the struggle after the Infinite, the reaching-out for the Supersensuous, as impracticable and absurd, and, in the same breath, asks us to take up ethics and do good to society. Why should we do good? Doing good is a secondary consideration. We must have an ideal. Ethics itself is not the end, but the means to the end.

If the end is not there, why should we be ethical? Why should I do good to other men, and not injure them? If happiness is the goal of mankind, why should I not make myself happy and others unhappy? What prevents me?

In modern times, too, the attempts made to preach religions without appealing to the supersensuous state if the mind have had to take up the old abstractions of the Ancients and give different names to them as "Moral Law", the "Ideal Unity", and so forth, thus showing that these abstractions are not in the senses. None of us have yet seen an "Ideal Human Being", and yet we are told to believe in it. None of us have yet seen an ideally perfect man, and yet without that ideal we cannot progress.

Thus, this one fact stands out from all these different religions, that there is an Ideal Unit Abstraction, which is put before us, either in the form of a Person or an Impersonal Being, or a Law, or a Presence, or an Essence. We are always struggling to raise ourselves up to that ideal.

Every human being, whosoever and wheresoever he may be, has an ideal of infinite power. Every human being has an ideal of infinite pleasure. Most of the works that we find around us, the activities displayed everywhere, are due to the struggle for this infinite power or this infinite pleasure.

But a few quickly discover that although they are struggling for infinite power, it is not through the senses that it can be reached. They find out very soon that that infinite pleasure is not to be got through the senses, or, in other words, the senses are too limited, and the body is too limited, to express the Infinite.

To manifest the Infinite through the finite is impossible, and sooner or later, man learns to give up the attempt to express the Infinite through the finite. This giving up, this renunciation of the attempt, is the background of ethics. Renunciation is the very basis upon which ethics stands. There never was an ethical code preached which had not renunciation for its basis.

Two birds of beautiful plumage, inseparable companions, sat upon the same tree, one on the top and one below. The beautiful bird below was eating the fruits of the tree, sweet and bitter, one moment a sweet one and another a bitter. The moment he ate a bitter fruit, he was sorry, but after a while he ate another and when it too was bitter, he looked up and saw the other bird who ate neither the sweet nor the bitter, but was calm and majestic, immersed in his own glory.

And then the poor lower bird forgot and went on eating the sweet and bitter fruits again, until at last he ate one that was extremely bitter; and then he stopped again and once more looked up at the glorious bird above. Then he came nearer and nearer to the other bird; and when he had come near enough, rays of light shone upon him and enveloped him, and he saw he was transformed into the higher bird.

He became calm, majestic, free, and found that there had been but one bird all the time on the tree. The lower bird was but the reflection of the one above.

So we are in reality one with the Lord, but the reflection makes us seem many, as when the one sun reflects in a million dew-drops and seems a million tiny suns. The reflection must vanish if we are to identify ourselves with our real nature which is divine. The universe itself can never be the limit of our satisfaction.

That is why the miser gathers more and more money, that is why the robber robs, the sinner sins, that is why you are learning philosophy. All have one purpose. There is no other purpose in life, save to reach this freedom. Consciously or unconsciously, we are all striving for perfection. Every being must attain to it.

And what becomes of a man when he attains perfection? He lives a life of bliss infinite. He enjoys infinite and perfect bliss, having obtained the only thing in which man ought to have pleasure, namely God, and enjoys the bliss with God.

This is the common religion of all the sects of India; but, then, perfection is absolute, and the absolute cannot be two or three. It cannot have any qualities. It cannot be an individual.

And so when a soul becomes perfect and absolute, it must become one with Brahman, and it would only realise the Lord as the perfection, the reality, of its own nature and existence, the existence absolute, knowledge absolute, and bliss absolute. We have often and often read this called the losing of individuality and becoming a stock or a stone.

"He jests at scars that never felt a wound."

I tell you it is nothing of the kind. If it is happiness to enjoy the consciousness of this small body, it must be greater happiness to enjoy the consciousness of two bodies, the measure of happiness increasing with the consciousness of an increasing number of bodies, the aim, the ultimate of happiness being reached when it would become a universal consciousness.

Therefore, to gain this infinite universal individuality, this miserable little prison-individuality must go. Then alone can death cease when I am alone with life, then alone can misery cease when I am one with happiness itself, then alone can all errors cease when I am one with knowledge itself; and this is the necessary scientific conclusion.

Science has proved to me that physical individuality is a delusion, that really my body is one little continuously changing body in an unbroken ocean of matter; and Advaita (unity) is the necessary conclusion with my other counterpart, soul.

Science is nothing but the finding of unity. As soon as science would reach perfect unity, it would stop from further progress, because it would reach the goal. Thus Chemistry could not progress farther when it would discover one element out of which all other could be made. Physics would stop when it would be able to fulfil its services in discovering one energy of which all others are but manifestations, and the science of religion become perfect when it would discover Him who is the one life in a universe of death, Him who is the constant basis of an ever-changing world.

One who is the only Soul of which all souls are but delusive manifestations. Thus is it, through multiplicity and duality, that the ultimate unity is reached. Religion can go no farther. This is the goal of all science.

All science is bound to come to this conclusion in the long run. Manifestation, and not creation, is the word of science today, and the Hindu is only glad that what he has been cherishing in his bosom for ages is going to be taught in more forcible language, and with further light from the latest conclusions of science.

Descend we now from the aspirations of philosophy to the religion of the ignorant. At the very outset, I may tell you that there is no polytheism in India. In every temple, if one stands by and listens, one will find the worshippers applying all the attributes of God, including omnipresence, to the images.

It is not polytheism, nor would the name henotheism explain the situation. "The rose called by any other name would smell as sweet." Names are not explanations.

I remember, as a boy, hearing a Christian missionary preach to a crowd in India. Among other sweet things he was telling them was that if he gave a blow to their idol with his stick, what could it do? One of his hearers sharply answered, "If I abuse your God, what can He do?" "You would be punished," said the preacher, "when you die." "So my idol will punish you when you die," retorted the Hindu.

The tree is known by its fruits. When I have seen amongst them that are called idolaters, men, the like of whom in morality and spirituality and love I have never seen anywhere, I stop and ask myself, "Can sin beget holiness?"

Superstition is a great enemy of man, but bigotry is worse. Why does a Christian go to church? Why is the cross holy? Why is the face turned toward the sky in prayer? Why are there so many images in the Catholic Church? Why are there so many images in the minds of Protestants when they pray?

My brethren, we can no more think about anything without a mental image than we can live without breathing. By the law of association, the material image calls up the mental idea and vice versa.

This is why the Hindu uses an external symbol when he worships. He will tell you it helps to keep his mind fixed on the Being to whom he prays. He knows as well as you do that the image is not God, is not omnipresent.

After all, how much does omnipresence mean to almost the whole world? It stands merely as a word, a symbol. Has God superficial area? If not, when we repeat that word "omnipresent", we think of the extended sky or of space, that is all.

As we find that somehow or other, by the laws of our mental constitution, we have to associate our ideas of infinity with the image of the blue sky, or of the sea, so we naturally connect our idea of holiness with the image of a church, a mosque, or a cross. The Hindus have associated the idea of holiness, purity, truth, omnipresence, and such other ideas with different images and forms.

But with this difference that while some people devote their whole lives to their idol of a church and never rise higher, because with them religion means an intellectual assent to certain doctrines and doing good to their fellows, the whole religion of the Hindu is centred in realisation. Man is to become divine by realising the divine. Idols or temples or churches or books are only the supports, the helps, of his spiritual childhood: but on and on he must progress.

He must not stop anywhere. "External worship, material worship, " say the scriptures, "is the lowest stage; struggling to rise high, mental prayer is the next stage, but the highest stage is when the Lord has been realised."

Mark, the same earnest man who is kneeling before the idol tells you, "Him the Sun cannot express, nor the moon, nor the stars, the lightning cannot express Him, nor what we speak of as fire; through Him they shine." But he does not abuse any one's idol or call its worship sin. He recognises in it a necessary stage of life. "The child is father of the man." Would it be right for an old man to say that childhood is a sin or youth a sin?

If a man can realise his divine nature with the help of an image, would it be right to call that a sin? Nor even when he has passed that stage, should he call it an error.

To the Hindu, man is not travelling from error to truth, but from truth to truth, from lower to higher truth. To him all the religions, from the lowest fetishism to the highest absolutism, mean so many attempts of the human soul to grasp and realise the Infinite, each determined by the conditions of its birth and association, and each of these marks a stage of progress; and every soul is a young eagle soaring higher and higher, gathering more and more strength, till it reaches the Glorious Sun.

Unity in variety is the plan of nature, and the Hindu has recognised it. Every other religion lays down certain fixed dogmas, and tries to force society to adopt them. It places before society only one coat which must fit Jack and John and Henry, all alike. If it does not fit John or Henry, he must go without a coat to cover his body. The Hindus have discovered that the absolute can only be realised, or thought of, or stated, through the relative, and the images, crosses, and crescents are simply so many symbols — so many pegs to hang the spiritual ideas on. It is not that this help is necessary for every one, but those that do not need it have no right to say that it is wrong. Nor is it compulsory in Hinduism.

Manifest Your Inward Power

Whatever you believe, that you will be. If you believe yourselves to be sages, sages you will be tomorrow. There is nothing to obstruct you.

For if there is one common doctrine that runs through all our apparently fighting and contradictory sects, it is that all glory, power, and purity are within the soul already; only according to Ramanuja, the soul contracts and expands at times, and according to Shankara, it comes under a delusion. Never mind these differences. All admit the truth that the power is there — potential or manifest it is there — and the sooner you believe that, the better for you.

All power is within you; you can do anything and everything. Believe in that; do not believe that you are weak; do not believe that you are half-crazy lunatics as most of us believe now-a-days. You can do anything and everything, without even the guidance of any one.

All the powers in the universe are already ours. It is we who have put our hands before our eyes and cry that it is dark. Know that there is no darkness around us. Take the hands away and there is the light which was from the beginning. Darkness never existed, weakness never existed. We who are fools cry that we are weak; we who are fools cry that we are impure.

Advance like a hero. Don't be thwarted by anything. How many days will this body last, with its happiness and misery? When you have got the human body, then rouse the Atman within and say — I have reached the state of fearlessness! Say — I am the Atman in which my lower ego has become merged for ever.

Be perfect in this idea; and then as long as the body endures, speak unto others this message of fearlessness: "Thou art That", "Arise, awake, and stop not till the goal is reached!" If you can achieve this, then shall I know that you are really a tenacious East Bengal man.

If there is sincerity of spirit, I tell you, for a certainty, you will attain self-realization in this very life. But manly endeavour is wanted. Do you know what it is? "I shall certainly attain Self-knowledge. Whatever obstacles may come, I shall certainly overcome them" — a firm determination like this is Purushakara.

"Whether my mother, father, friends, brothers, wife, and children live or die, whether this body remains or goes, I shall never turn back till I attain to the vision of the Atman" — this resolute endeavour to advance towards one's goal, setting at naught all other considerations, is termed manly endeavour.

Otherwise, endeavour for creature comforts even beasts and birds show. Man has got this body simply to realise Self-knowledge. If you follow the common run of people in the world and float with the general current, where then is your manliness? Well, the common people are going to the jaws of death! But you have come to conquer it!

All great undertakings are achieved through mighty obstacles. — You valiant one, put forth your manly efforts; Wretched people under the grip of lust and gold deserve to be looked upon with indifference.

Apply to the service of the Lord that active impulse of manliness which your eagerness to help me through brotherly love has brought out in you. Do not open out your mind, unless you feel it will be positively beneficial. Use agreeable and wholesome language towards even the greatest enemy.

The desire for fame, for riches, for enjoyment is quite natural to every mortal, dear brother, and if that agrees well with serving both ways (i.e. serving both God and mammon), why, all men would exhibit great zeal! It is only the great saint who can work, making a mountain of an atom of virtue in others and cherishing no desire but that of the good of the world

All knowledge is within us. All perfection is there already in the soul. But this perfection has been covered up by nature; layer after layer of nature is covering this purity of the soul. What have we to do? Really we do not develop our souls at all. What can develop the perfect? We simply take the evil off; and the soul manifests itself in its pristine purity, its natural, innate freedom.

All noble undertakings are fraught with obstacles. It is quite in the nature of things. Keep up the deepest mental poise. Take not even the slightest notice of what puerile creatures may be saying against you. Indifference, indifference, indifference!

All search is vain, until we begin to perceive that knowledge is within ourselves, that no one can help us, that we must help ourselves.

All the misery we have is of our own choosing; such is our nature. The old Chinaman, who having been kept in prison for sixty years was released on the coronation of a new emperor, exclaimed, when he came out, that he could not live; he must go back to his horrible dungeon among the rats and mice; he could not bear the light. So he asked them to kill him or send him back to the prison, and he was sent back.

Exactly similar is the condition of all men. We run headlong after all sorts of misery, and are unwilling to be freed from them. Every day we run after pleasure, and before we reach it, we find it is gone, it has slipped through our fingers. Still we do not cease from our mad pursuit, but on and on we go, blinded fools that we are.

Vedanta not only insists that the ideal is practical, but that it has been so all the time; and this Ideal, this Reality, is our own nature. Everything else that you see is false, untrue. As soon as you say, "I am a little mortal being," you are saying something which is not true, you are giving the lie to yourselves, you are hypnotising yourselves into something vile and weak and wretched.

The Vedanta recognises no sin, it only recognises error. And the greatest error, says the Vedanta, is to say that you are weak, that you are a sinner, a miserable creature, and that you have no power and you cannot do this and that. Every time you think in that way, you, as it were, rivet one more link in the chain that binds you down, you add one more layer of hypnotism on to your own soul.

Therefore, whosoever thinks he is weak is wrong, whosoever thinks he is impure is wrong, and is throwing a bad thought into the world. This we must always bear in mind that in the Vedanta there is no attempt at reconciling the present life — the hypnotised life, this false life which we have assumed — with the ideal; but this false life must go, and the real life which is always existing must manifest itself, must shine out.

No man becomes purer and purer, it is a matter of greater manifestation. The veil drops away, and the native purity of the soul begins to manifest itself. Everything is ours already — infinite purity, freedom, love, and power.

The Vedanta also says that not only can this be realised in the depths of forests or caves, but by men in all possible conditions of life. We have seen that the people who discovered these truths were neither living in caves nor forests, nor following the ordinary vocations of life, but men who, we have every reason to believe, led the busiest of lives, men who had to command armies, to sit on thrones, and look to the welfare of millions — and all these, in the days of absolute monarchy, and not as in these days when a king is to a great extent a mere figurehead.

Yet they could find time to think out all these thoughts, to realise them, and to teach them to humanity. How much more then should it be practical for us whose lives, compared with theirs, are lives of leisure? That we cannot realise them is a shame to us, seeing that we are comparatively free all the time, having very little to do.

My requirements are as nothing compared with those of an ancient absolute monarch. My wants are as nothing compared with the demands of Arjuna on the battlefield of Kurukshetra, commanding a huge army; and yet he could find time in the midst of the din and turmoil of battle to talk the highest philosophy and to carry it into his life also. Surely we ought to be able to do as much in this life of ours — comparatively free, easy, and comfortable.

Most of us here have more time than we think we have, if we really want to use it for good. With the amount of freedom we have we can attain to two hundred ideals in this life, if we will, but we must not degrade the ideal to the actual.

One of the most insinuating things comes to us in the shape of persons who apologise for our mistakes and teach us how to make special excuses for all our foolish wants and foolish desires; and we think that their ideal is the only ideal we need have. But it is not so. The Vedanta teaches no such thing. The actual should be reconciled to the ideal, the present life should be made to coincide with life eternal.

"Arise, awake, sleep no more; within each of you there is the power to remove all wants and all miseries. Believe this, and that power will be manifested.

Avoid weakness and slavery.

Look at the "ocean" and not at the "wave"; see no difference between ant and angel. Every worm is the brother of the Nazarene. How say one is greater and one less? Each is great in his own place.

We are in the sun and in the stars as much as here. Spirit is beyond space and time and is everywhere. Every mouth praising the Lord is my mouth, every eye seeing is my eye.

We are confined nowhere; we are not body, the universe is our body. We are magicians waving magic wands and creating scenes before us at will. We are the spider in his huge web, who can go on the varied strands wheresoever he desires. The spider is now only conscious of the spot where he is, but he will in time become conscious of the whole web.

We are now conscious only where the body is, we can use only one brain; but when we reach ultraconsciousness, we know all, we can use all brains. Even now we can "give the push" in consciousness, and it goes beyond and acts in the superconscious.

We are striving "to be" and nothing more, no "I" ever — just pure crystal, reflecting all, but ever the same, When that state is reached, there is no more doing; the body becomes a mere mechanism, pure without care for it; it cannot become impure.

Know you are the Infinite, then fear must die. Say ever, "I and my Father are one."

Awake, awake, great ones! The world is burning with misery. Can you sleep? Let us call and call till the sleeping gods awake, till the god within answers to the call. What more is in life? What greater work? The details come to me as I go. I never make plans. Plans grow and work themselves. I only say, awake, awake!

Be brave and be sincere; then follow any path with devotion, and you must reach the Whole. Once lay hold of one link of the chain, and the whole chain must come by degrees.

Be free; hope for nothing from anyone. I am sure if you look back upon your lives you will find that you were always vainly trying to get help from others which never came.

Be perfectly unselfish, be steady and work on. We will do great things; do not fear... One thing more. Be the servant of all, and do not try in the least to govern others. That will excite jealousy and destroy everything... Go on. You have worked wonderfully well. We do not wait for help, we will work it out, my boy, be self-reliant, faithful and patient. Do not antagonise my other friends, live in harmony with all. My eternal love to all.

Be perfectly resigned, perfectly unconcerned; then alone can you do any true work. No eyes can see the real forces; we can only see the results. Put out self, forget it; just let God work, it is His business.

Being reminded of weakness does not help much; give strength, and strength does not come by thinking of weakness all the time. The remedy for weakness is not brooding over weakness, but thinking of strength.

Blame neither man, nor God, nor anyone in the world. When you find yourselves suffering, blame yourselves, and try to do better.

Calm and silent and steady work, and no newspaper humbug, no name-making, you must always remember.

Come out into the broad light of day, come out from the little narrow paths, for how can the infinite soul rest content to live and die in small ruts?

Each one of us reaps what we ourselves have sown. These miseries under which we suffer, these bondages under which we struggle, have been caused by ourselves, and none else in the universe is to blame. God is the least to blame for it.

Each person tries to hold himself faultless and lay the blame upon somebody or something else, or even on bad luck.

Even at the gate of death, in the greatest danger, in the thick of the battlefield, at the bottom of the ocean, on the tops of the highest mountains, in the thickest of the forest, tell yourself, “I am He, I am He”. Day and night say, “I am He”. It is the greatest strength; it is religion.

Help does not come from without; it comes from within ourselves. Cry to all the gods in the universe. I cried for years, and in the end I found that I was helped. But help came from within.

It is fear alone that is death. You have to go beyond all fear. So from this day be fearless.

Let people say whatever they like, stick to your own convictions, and rest assured, the world will be at your feet. They say, ‘Have faith in this fellow or that fellow’, but, I say, ‘Have faith in yourself first’. that’s the way.

Let us be true. Nine-tenths of our life's energy is spent in trying to make people think us that which we are not. That energy would be more rightly spent in becoming that which we would like to be.

Let us proclaim to every soul: उत्तिष्ठत जाग्रत प्राप्य वरान्निबोधत — Arise, awake, and stop not till the goal is reached. Arise, awake! Awake from this hypnotism of weakness.

Mark you, let us all be honest. If we cannot follow the ideal, let us confess our weakness, but not degrade it; let not any try to pull it down.

No great thing can be done without sacrifice.

Nobody will come to help you if you put yourself forward as a leader.Kill self first if you want to succeed.

Nothing else is necessary but these — love, sincerity, and patience.

Persevere on, my brave lads, We have only just begun. Never despond! Never say enough!

So'ham — I am He. Repeat the idea constantly, voluntarily at first; then it becomes automatic in practice. It percolates to the nerves. So this idea, by rote, by repetition, should be driven even into the nerves.

Struggle hard and then if you do not succeed, you are not to blame. Let the world praise or blame you. Let all the wealth of the earth come to your feet, or let you be made the poorest on earth. Let death come this moment or hundreds of years hence. Swerve not from the path you have taken. All good thoughts are immortal and go to make Buddhas and Christs.

Struggle, struggle, was my motto for the last ten years. Struggle, still say I. When it was all dark, I used to say, struggle; when light is breaking in, I still say, struggle. Be not afraid, my children. Look not up in that attitude of fear towards that infinite starry vault as if it would crush you.

Take care! Beware of everything that is untrue; stick to truth and we shall succeed, maybe slowly, but surely.

Take courage and work on. Patience and steady work — this is the only way. Go on; remember — patience and purity and courage and steady work. . . . So long as you are pure, and true to your principles, you will never fail.

Take up one idea. Make that one idea your life — think of it, dream of it, live on that idea. Let the brain, muscles, nerves, every part of your body, be full of that idea, and just leave every other idea alone. This is the way to success.

The brave alone can afford to be sincere. Compare the lion and the fox.

The whole secret of existence is to have no fear. Never fear what will become of you.

This is the first lesson to learn: be determined not to curse anything outside, not to lay the blame upon any one outside, but be a man, stand up, lay the blame on yourself. You will find, that is always true. Get hold of yourself.

Those who die, merely suffering the woes of life like cats and dogs, are they men? He is a man who even when agitated by the sharp interaction of pleasure and pain is discriminating, and knowing them to be of an evanescent nature, becomes passionately devoted to the Atman. This is all the difference between men and animals.

Truth, purity, and unselfishness — wherever these are present, there is no power below or above the sun to crush the possessor thereof. Equipped with these, one individual is able to face the whole universe in opposition.

We are forever trying to make our weakness look like strength, our sentiment like love, our cowardice like courage, etc. Say to your soul in regard to vanities, weaknesses, etc., “This does not befit thee. This does not befit thee”.

Whatever you believe, that you will be. If you believe yourselves to be sages, sages you will be tomorrow. There is nothing to obstruct you.

You are a part of the Infinite. This is your nature. Hence you are your brother’s keeper… When you hurt anyone you hurt yourself, for you and your brother are one.

You have to grow from the inside out. None can teach you, none can make you spiritual. There is no other teacher but your own soul.

You must have an iron will if you would cross the ocean. You must be strong enough to pierce mountains.

Be free; hope for nothing from anyone. I am sure if you look back upon your lives you will find that you were always vainly trying to get help from others which never came.

Be not afraid, for all great power throughout the history of humanity has been with the people. From out of their ranks have come all the greatest geniuses of the world, and history can only repeat itself. Be not afraid of anything. You will do marvellous work.

Be not in despair, the way is very difficult, like walking on the edge of a razor; yet despair not, arise, awake, and find the ideal, the goal.

Be strong, my young friends; that is my advice to you. You will be nearer to Heaven through football than through the study of the Gita. These are bold words; but I have to say them, for I love you. I know where the shoe pinches.

Calm and silent and steady work, and no newspaper humbug, no name-making, you must always remember.

Come out into the broad open light of day, come out from the little narrow paths, for how can the infinite soul rest content to live and die in small ruts? Come out into the universe of Light. Everything in the universe is yours, stretch out your arms and embrace it with love. If you ever felt you wanted to do that, you have felt God.

Cowards only sin, brave men never, no, not even in mind.

Do not be afraid of a small beginning. great things come afterwards. Be courageous. Do not try to lead your brethren, but serve them. The brutal mania for leading has sunk many a great ships in the waters of life. Take care especially of that, i.e. be unselfish even unto death, and work.

Do not figure out big plans at first, but, begin slowly, feel your ground and proceed up and up.

Do not wait for anybody or anything. Do whatever you can. Build your hope on none.

Go on bravely. Do not expect success in a day or a year. Always hold on to the highest. Be steady. Avoid jealousy and selfishness. Be obedient and eternally faithful to the cause of truth, humanity, and your country, and you will move the world.

Have faith in yourselves, and stand up on that faith and be strong; that is what we need.

Hold on to your own ideal. . . . Above all, never attempt to guide or rule others, or, as the Yankees say, "boss" others. Be the servant of all.

I hate cowardice; I will have nothing to do with cowards or political nonsense. I do not believe in any politics. God and truth are the only politics in the world, everything else is trash.

I want each one of my children to be a hundred times greater than I could ever be. Everyone of you must be a giant—must, that is my word. Obedience, readiness, and love for the cause— if you have these three, nothing can hold you back.

If you are really my children, you will fear nothing, stop at nothing. You will be like lions. We must rouse India and the whole world. No cowardice. I will take no nay. Do you understand?

If you can think that infinite power, infinite knowledge and indomitable energy lie within you, and if you can bring out that power, you also can become like me.

Infinite patience, infinite purity, and infinite perseverance are the secret of success in a good cause.

It is our own mental attitude which makes the world what it is for us. Our thoughts make things beautiful, our thoughts make things ugly. The whole world is in our own minds. Learn to see things in the proper light.

Know that every time you feel weak, you not only hurt yourself but also the cause. Infinite faith and strength are the only conditions of success.

Let people say whatever they like, stick to your own convictions, and rest assured, the world will be at your feet. They say, 'Have faith in this fellow or that fellow', but, I say, 'Have faith in yourself first'. that's the way.

We are responsible for what we are, and whatever we wish ourselves to be, we have the power to make ourselves. If what we are now has been the result of our own past actions, it certainly follows that whatever we wish to be in future can be produced by our present actions; so we have to know how to act.

We are what our thoughts have made us; so take care about what you think. Words are secondary. Thoughts live; they travel far.

We reap what we sow. We are the makers of our own fate. None else has the blame, none has the praise.

Whatever you think, that you will be. If you think yourselves weak, weak you will be; if you think yourselves strong, strong you will be; if you think yourselves impure, impure you will be; if you think yourselves pure, pure you will be.

Blame none for your own faults, stand upon your own feet, and take the whole responsibility upon yourselves. Say, "This misery that I am suffering is of my own doing, and that very thing proves that it will have to be undone by me alone." That which I created, I can demolish; that which is created by some one else I shall never be able to destroy. Therefore, stand up, be bold, be strong. Take the whole responsibility on your own shoulders, and know that you are the creator of your own destiny.

Bold words and bolder deeds are what we want. Awake, awake, great ones! The world is burning with misery. Can you sleep? Let us call and call till the sleeping gods awake, till the god within answers to the call. What more is in life? What greater work? The details come to me as I go. I never make plans. Plans grow and work themselves. I only say, awake, awake!

The Practice of Concentration

Concentration, of course, comes from various sources. Through the senses you can get concentration. Some get it when they hear beautiful music, others when they see beautiful scenery. Some get concentrated by lying upon beds of spikes, sharp iron spikes, others by sitting upon sharp pebbles. These are extraordinary cases using most unscientific procedure. Scientific procedure is gradually training the mind.

One gets concentrated by holding his arm up. Torture gives him the concentration he wants. But all these are extraordinary.

Universal methods have been organised according to different philosophers. Some say the state we want to attain is super-consciousness of the mind — going beyond the limitations the body has made for us. The value of ethics to the Yogi lies in that it makes the mind pure. The purer the mind, the easier it is to control it. The mind takes every thought that rises and works it out. The grosser the mind, the more difficult it is to control it. The immoral man will never be able to concentrate his mind to study psychology. He may get a little control as he begins, get a little power of hearing. and even those powers will go from him. The difficulty is that if you study closely, you see how the extraordinary power arrived at was not attained by regular scientific training. The men who, by the power of magic, control serpents will be killed by serpents. The man who attains any extraordinary powers will in the long run succumb to those powers. There are millions who receive power through all sorts of ways in India. The vast majority of them die raving lunatics. Quite a number commit suicide, the mind being unbalanced.

The study must be put on the safe side: scientific, slow, peaceful. The first requisite is to be moral. Such a man wants the gods to come down, and they will come down and manifest themselves to him. That is our psychology and philosophy in essence, to be perfectly moral. Just think what that means! No injury, perfect purity, perfect austerity! These are absolutely necessary. Just think, if a man can attain all these in perfection! What more do you want? If he is free from all enmity towards any being, all animals will give up their enmity in his presence. The Yogis lay down very strict laws so that one cannot pass off for a charitable man without being charitable.

The law of laws is concentration. First, concentrate all the nerve energies and all power lodged in the cells of the body into one force and direct it at will. Then bring the mind, which is thinner matter, into one centre. The mind has layer after layer. When the nerve force concentrated is made to pass through the spinal column, one layer of the mind is open. When it is concentrated in one bone plexus, or "lotus", another part of the world is open. So from world to world it goes until it touches the pineal gland in the centre of the brain. This is the seat of conservation of potential energy, the source of both activity and passivity.

No one method can suit all. Different methods are not steps necessary to be taken one after another. Ceremonials are the lowest form; next God external, and after that God internal. In some cases gradation may be needed, but in many only one way is required. It would be the height of folly to say to everyone, "You must pass through Karma and Bhakti before you can reach Jnana."

Stick to your reason until you reach something higher; and you will know it to be higher, because it will not jar with reason. The stage beyond consciousness is inspiration (Samadhi); but never mistake hysterical trances for the real thing.

It is a terrible thing to claim this inspiration falsely, to mistake instinct for inspiration. There is no external test for inspiration, we know it ourselves; our guardian against mistake is negative — the voice of reason. All religion is going beyond reason, but reason is the only guide to get there.

Instinct is like ice, reason is the water, and inspiration is the subtlest form or vapour; one follows the other. Everywhere is this eternal sequence — unconsciousness, consciousness, intelligence — matter, body, mind — and to us it seems as if the chain began with the particular link we first lay hold of. Arguments on both sides are of equal weight, and both are true. We must reach beyond both, to where there is neither the one nor the other. These successions are all Maya.

It is easy to concentrate the mind on external things, the mind naturally goes outwards; but not so in the case of religion, or psychology, or metaphysics, where the subject and the object, are one. The object is internal, the mind itself is the object, and it is necessary to study the mind itself — mind studying mind. We know that there is the power of the mind called reflection. I am talking to you. At the same time I am standing aside, as it were, a second person, and knowing and hearing what I am talking. You work and think at the same time, while a portion of your mind stands by and sees what you are thinking. The powers of the mind should be concentrated and turned back upon itself, and as the darkest places reveal their secrets before the penetrating rays of the sun, so will this concentrated mind penetrate its own innermost secrets. Thus will we come to the basis of belief, the real genuine religion. We will perceive for ourselves whether we have souls, whether life is of five minutes or of eternity, whether there is a God in the universe or more. It will all be revealed to us. This is what Raja-Yoga proposes to teach. The goal of all its teaching is how to concentrate the minds, then, how to discover the innermost recesses of our own minds, then, how to generalise their contents and form our own conclusions from them. It, therefore, never asks the question what our religion is, whether we are Deists or Atheists, whether Christians, Jews, or Buddhists. We are human beings; that is sufficient. Every human being has the right and the power to seek for religion. Every human being has the right to ask the reason, why, and to have his question answered by himself, if he only takes the trouble.

So far, then, we see that in the study of this Raja-Yoga no faith or belief is necessary. Believe nothing until you find it out for yourself; that is what it teaches us.

Do you mean to say that the facts of our awakened state require any dreams or imaginings to prove them? Certainly not. This study of Raja-Yoga takes a long time and constant practice. A part of this practice is physical, but in the main it is mental. As we proceed we shall find how intimately the mind is connected with the body. If we believe that the mind is simply a finer part of the body, and that mind acts upon the body, then it stands to reason that the body must react upon the mind. If the body is sick, the mind becomes sick also. If the body is healthy, the mind remains healthy and strong. When one is angry, the mind becomes disturbed. Similarly when the mind is disturbed, the body also becomes disturbed. With the majority of mankind the mind is greatly under the control of the body, their mind being very little developed. The vast mass of humanity is very little removed from the animals. Not only so, but in many instances, the power of control in them is little higher than that of the lower animals. We have very little command of our minds. Therefore to bring that command about, to get that control over body and mind, we must take certain physical helps. When the body is sufficiently controlled, we can attempt the manipulation of the mind. By manipulating the mind, we shall be able to bring it under our control, make it work as we like, and compel it to concentrate its powers as we desire.

The Importance of Concentration

All knowledge that we have, either of the external or internal world, is obtained through only one method — by the concentration of the mind. No knowledge can be had of any science unless we can concentrate our minds upon the subject. The astronomer concentrates his mind through the telescope and so on. If you want to study your own mind, it will be the same process. You will have to concentrate your mind and turn it back upon itself. The difference in this world between mind and mind is simply the fact of concentration. One, more concentrated than the other, gets more knowledge.

Concentration is the essence of all knowledge, nothing can be done without it. Ninety per cent of thought force is wasted by the ordinary human being, and therefore he is constantly committing blunders; the trained man or mind never makes a mistake. Concentration is restraining the mind into smaller and smaller limits.

When the mind is concentrated and turned backward on itself, all within us will be our servants, not our masters. The Greeks applied their concentration to the external world, and the result was perfection in art, literature, etc. The Hindu concentrated on the internal world, upon the unseen realms in the Self, and developed the science of Yoga.

Yoga is controlling the senses, will and mind. The benefit of its study is that we learn to control instead of being controlled.

Mind seems to be layer on layer. Our real goal is to cross all these intervening strata of our being and find God. The end and aim of Yoga is to realise God.

To do this we must go beyond relative knowledge, go beyond the sense-world. The world is awake to the senses, the children of the Lord are asleep on that plane. The world is asleep to the Eternal, the children of the Lord are awake in that realm. These are the sons of God.

There is but one way to control the senses — to see Him who is the Reality in the universe. Then and only then can we really conquer our senses.

The more this power of concentration, the more knowledge is acquired, because this is the one and only method of acquiring knowledge. Even the lowest shoeblack, if he gives more concentration, will black shoes better; the cook with concentration will cook a meal all the better.

In making money, or in worshipping God, or in doing anything, the stronger the power of concentration, the better will that thing be done. This is the one call, the one knock, which opens the gates of nature, and lets out floods of light. This, the power of concentration, is the only key to the treasure-house of knowledge.

How are we to know that the mind has become concentrated? Because the idea of time will vanish. The more time passes unnoticed the more concentrated we are.

In common life we see that when we are interested in a book we do not note the time at all; and when we leave the book, we are often surprised to find how many hours have passed. All time will have the tendency to come and stand in the one present.

So the definition is given: When the past and present come and stand in one, the mind is said to be concentrated.

We read many books, but that does not bring us knowledge. We may read all the Bibles in the world, but that will not give us religion. Theoretical religion is easy enough to get, any one may get that. What we want is practical religion.

The Christian idea of a practical religion is in doing good works — worldly utility.

What good is utility? Judged from a utilitarian standpoint, religion is a failure. Every hospital is a prayer that more people may come there.

What is meant by charity? Charity is not fundamental. It is really helping on the misery of the world, not eradicating it. One looks for name and fame and covers his efforts to obtain them with the enamel of charity and good works. He is working for himself under the pretext of working for others. Every so-called charity is an encouragement of the very evil it claims to operate against.

Men and women go to balls and dance all night in honour of some hospital or other charitable institution then go home, behave like beasts, and bring devils into the world to fill jails, insane asylums, and hospitals. So it goes on, and it is called good works — building hospital etc.

The ideal of good works is to lessen, or eradicate, the misery of the world. The Yogi says, all misery comes from not being able to control the mind. The Yogi's ideal is freedom from nature. Conquest of nature is his standard of work. The Yogi says that all power is in the soul, and by the controlling of the mind and body one conquers nature by the power of the soul.

How has all the knowledge in the world been gained but by the concentration of the powers of the mind? The world is ready to give up its secrets if we only know how to knock, how to give it the necessary blow.

The strength and force of the blow come through concentration. There is no limit to the power of the human mind. The more concentrated it is, the more power is brought to bear on one point; that is the secret.

It is impossible to find God outside of ourselves. Our own souls contribute all the divinity that is outside of us. We are the greatest temple. The objectification is only a faint imitation of what we see within ourselves.

Concentration of the powers of the mind is our only instrument to help us see God. If you know one soul (your own), you know all souls, past, present, and to come.

The will concentrates the mind, certain things excite and control this will, such as reason, love, devotion, breathing. The concentrated mind is a lamp that shows us every corner of the soul.

The main difference between men and the animals is the difference in their power of concentration. All success in any line of work is the result of this.

Everybody knows something about concentration. We see its results every day. High achievements in art, music, etc., are the results of concentration.

An animal has very little power of concentration. Those who have trained animals find much difficulty in the fact that the animal is constantly forgetting what is told him. He cannot concentrate his mind long upon anything at a time. Herein is the difference between man and the animals — man has the greater power of concentration.

The difference in their power of concentration also constitutes the difference between man and man. Compare the lowest with the highest man. The difference is in the degree of concentration. This is the only difference.

Everybody's mind becomes concentrated at times. We all concentrate upon those things we love, and we love those things upon which we concentrate our minds.

What mother is there that does not love the face of her homeliest child? That face is to her the most beautiful in the world. She loves it because she concentrates her mind on it; and if every one could concentrate his mind on that same face, every one would love it. It would be to all the most beautiful face.

We all concentrate our minds upon those things we love. When we hear beautiful music, our minds become fastened upon it, and we cannot take them away. Those who concentrate their minds upon what you call classical music do not like common music, and vice versa. Music in which the notes follow each other in rapid succession holds the mind readily.

A child loves lively music, because the rapidity of the notes gives the mind no chance to wander. A man who likes common music dislikes classical music, because it is more complicated and requires a greater degree of concentration to follow it.

The great trouble with such concentrations is that we do not control the mind; it controls us. Something outside of ourselves, as it were, draws the mind into it and holds it as long as it chooses. We hear melodious tones or see a beautiful painting, and the mind is held fast! We cannot take it away.

If I speak to you well upon a subject you like, your mind becomes concentrated upon what I am saying. I draw your mind away from yourself and hold it upon the subject in spite of yourself. Thus our attention is held, our minds are concentrated upon various things, in spite of ourselves. We cannot help it.

Now the question is: Can this concentration be developed, and can we become masters of it? The Yogis say, yes. The Yogis say that we can get perfect control of the mind.

On the ethical side there is danger in the development of the power of concentration — the danger of concentrating the mind upon an object and then being unable to detach it at will. This state causes great suffering. Almost all our suffering is caused by our not having the power of detachment.

So along with the development of concentration we must develop the power of detachment. We must learn not only to attach the mind to one thing exclusively, but also to detach it at a moment's notice and place it upon something else. These two should be developed together to make it safe.

This is the systematic development of the mind. To me the very essence of education is concentration of mind, not the collecting of facts. If I had to do my education over again, and had any voice in the matter, I would not study facts at all. I would develop the power of concentration and detachment, and then with a perfect instrument I could collect facts at will. Side by side, in the child, should be developed the power of concentration and detachment.

In the lives of all great men, past and present, we find this tremendous power of concentration. Those are men of genius, you say. The science of Yoga tells us that we are all geniuses if we try hard to be. Some will come into this life better fitted and will do it quicker perhaps. We can all do the same. The same power is in everyone. The subject of the present lecture is how to concentrate the mind in order to study the mind itself. Yogis have laid down certain rules and this night I am going to give you a sketch of some of these rules.

The Spirit of Devotion to Duty

Each duty has its own place, and according to the circumstances in which we are placed, we must perform our duties. what is duty for one is not duty for another. At the same time, we do not say that this duty is lowering and the other elevating.

Isolation of the soul from all objects, mental and physical, is the goal; when that is attained, the soul will find that it was alone all the time, and it required no one to make it happy. As long as we require someone else to make us happy, we are slaves. When the Purusha finds that It is free, and does not require anything to complete Itself, that this nature is quite unnecessary, then freedom (Kaivalya) is attained.

Men run after a few dollars and do not think anything of cheating a fellow-being to get those dollars; but if they would restrain themselves, in a few years they would develop such characters as would bring them millions of dollars — if they wanted them. Then their will would govern the universe. But we are all such fools!

What is the use of talking of one's mistakes to the world? They cannot thereby be undone. For what one has done one must suffer; one must try and do better. The world sympathises only with the strong and the powerful.

It is only work that is done as a free-will offering to humanity and to nature that does not bring with it any binding attachment.

Duty of any kind is not to be slighted. A man who does the lower work is not, for that reason only, a lower man than he who does the higher work; a man should not be judged by the nature of his duties, but by the manner in which he does them. His manner of doing them and his power to do them are indeed the test of a man. A shoemaker who can turn out a strong, nice pair of shoes in the shortest possible time is a better man, according to his profession and his work, than a professor who talks nonsense every day of his life.

Every duty is holy, and devotion to duty is the highest form of the worship of God; it is certainly a source of great help in enlightening and emancipating the deluded and ignorance-encumbered souls of the Baddhas — the bound ones.

By doing well the duty which is nearest to us, the duty which is in our hands now, we make ourselves stronger and improving our strength in this manner step by step, we may even reach a state in which it shall be our privilege to do the most coveted and honoured duties in life and in society.

Our first duty is not to hate ourselves, because to advance we must have faith in ourselves first and then in God. He who has no faith in himself can never have faith in God. Therefore, the only alternative remaining to us is to recognise that duty and morality vary under different circumstances; not that the man who resists evil is doing what is always and in itself wrong, but that in the different circumstances in which he is placed it may become even his duty to resist evil.

All great teachers have taught, "Resist not evil," that non-resistance is the highest moral ideal. We all know that, if a certain number of us attempted to put that maxim fully into practice, the whole social fabric would fall to pieces, the wicked would take possession of our properties and our lives, and would do whatever they liked with us. Even if only one day of such non-resistance were practiced, it would lead to disaster.

Yet, intuitively, in our heart of hearts we feel the truth of the teaching "Resist not evil." This seems to us to be the highest ideal; yet to teach this doctrine only would be equivalent to condemning a vast portion of mankind.

Not only so, it would be making men feel that they were always doing wrong, and cause in them scruples of conscience in all their actions; it would weaken them, and that constant self-disapproval would breed more vice than any other weakness would. To the man who has begun to hate himself the gate to degeneration has already opened; and the same is true of a nation.

He who has no faith in himself can never have faith in God. Therefore, the only alternative remaining to us is to recognise that duty and morality vary under different circumstances; not that the man who resists evil is doing what is always and in itself wrong, but that in the different circumstances in which he is placed it may become even his duty to resist evil.

You should cultivate a noble nature by doing your duty. By doing our duty we get rid of the idea of duty; and then and then only we feel everything as done by God. We are but machines in His hand. This body is opaque, God is the lamp. Whatever is going out of the body is God's.

You do not feel it. You feel "I". This is delusion. You must learn calm submission to the will of God. Duty is the best school for it. This duty is morality.

Drill yourself to be thoroughly submissive. Get rid of the "I". No humbuggism. Then you can get rid of the idea of duty; for all is His. Then you go on naturally, forgiving, forgetting, etc.

Our religion always presents different gradations of duty and religion to different people.

Duty is seldom sweet. It is only when love greases its wheels that it runs smoothly; it is a continuous friction otherwise.

How else could parents do their duties to their children, husbands to their wives, and vice versa? Do we not meet with cases of friction every day in our lives? Duty is sweet only through love, and love shines in freedom alone.

Yet is it freedom to be a slave to the senses, to anger, to jealousies and a hundred other petty things that must occur every day in human life? In all these little roughnesses that we meet with in life, the highest expression of freedom is to forbear.

Women, slaves to their own irritable, jealous tempers, are apt to blame their husbands, and assert their own "freedom", as they think, not knowing that thereby they only prove that they are slaves. So it is with husbands who eternally find fault with their wives.

There is a sage in India, a great Yogi, one of the most wonderful men I have ever seen in my life. He is a peculiar man, he will not teach any one; if you ask him a question he will not answer. It is too much for him to take up the position of a teacher, he will not do it. If you ask a question, and wait for some days, in the course of conversation he will bring up the subject, and wonderful light will he throw on it.

He told me once the secret of work, "Let the end and the means be joined into one." When you are doing any work, do not think of anything beyond. Do it as worship, as the highest worship, and devote your whole life to it for the time being.

Thus, in the story, the Vyadha and the woman did their duty with cheerfulness and whole-heartedness; and the result was that they became illuminated, clearly showing that the right performance of the duties of any station in life, without attachment to results, leads us to the highest realisation of the perfection of the soul.

It is the worker who is attached to results that grumbles about the nature of the duty which has fallen to his lot. To the unattached worker all duties are equally good, and form efficient instruments with which selfishness and sensuality may be killed, and the freedom of the soul secured.

We are all apt to think too highly of ourselves. Our duties are determined by our desires to a much larger extent than we are willing to grant. Competition rouses envy, and it kills the kindliness of the heart. To the grumbler all duties are distasteful; nothing will ever satisfy him, and his whole life is doomed to prove a failure.

Let us work on, doing as we go whatever happens to be our duty, and being ever ready to put our shoulders to the wheel. Then surely shall we see the Light!

Karma-Yoga teaches us that the ordinary idea of duty is on the lower plane; nevertheless, all of us have to do our duty. Yet we may see that this peculiar sense of duty is very often a great cause of misery.

Duty becomes a disease with us; it drags us ever forward. It catches hold of us and makes our whole life miserable. It is the bane of human life. This duty, this idea of duty is the midday summer sun which scorches the innermost soul of mankind.

Look at those poor slaves to duty! Duty leaves them no time to say prayers, no time to bathe. Duty is ever on them. They go out and work. Duty is on them!

They come home and think of the work for the next day. Duty is on them! It is living a slave's life, at last dropping down in the street and dying in harness, like a horse.

This is duty as it is understood.

What is duty after all? It is really the impulsion of the flesh, of our attachment; and when an attachment has become established, we call it duty.

It is, so to say, a sort of chronic disease. When it is acute, we call it disease; when it is chronic, we call it nature. It is a disease.

So when attachment becomes chronic, we baptise it with the high sounding name of duty. We strew flowers upon it, trumpets sound for it, sacred texts are said over it, and then the whole world fights, and men earnestly rob each other for this duty's sake.

Duty is good to the extent that it checks brutality. To the lowest kinds of men, who cannot have any other ideal, it is of some good; but those who want to be Karma-Yogis must throw this idea of duty overboard. There is no duty for you and me. Whatever you have to give to the world, do give by all means, but not as a duty. Do not take any thought of that. Be not compelled.

Unity in variety is the plan of creation. However men and women may vary individually, there is unity in the background. The different individual characters and classes of men and women are natural variations in creation.

Hence, we ought not to judge them by the same standard or put the same ideal before them. Such a course creates only an unnatural struggle, and the result is that man begins to hate himself and is hindered from becoming religious and good. Our duty is to encourage every one in his struggle to live up to his own highest ideal, and strive at the same time to make the ideal as near as possible to the truth.

In the material physical world, expansion is life, and contraction is death. Whatever ceases to expand ceases to live. Translating this in the moral world we have: If one would expand, he must love, and when he ceases to love he dies. It is your nature; you must, because that is the only law of life.

Therefore, we must love God for love's sake, so we must do our duty for duty's sake; we must work for work's sake without looking for any reward — know that you are purer and more perfect, know that this is the real temple of God.

Every man should take up his own ideal and endeavour to accomplish it. That is a surer way of progress than taking up other men's ideals, which he can never hope to accomplish.

For instance, we take a child and at once give him the task of walking twenty miles. Either the little one dies, or one in a thousand crawls the twenty miles, to reach the end exhausted and half-dead.

That is like what we generally try to do with the world. All the men and women, in any society, are not of the same mind, capacity, or of the same power to do things; they must have different ideals, and we have no right to sneer at any ideal. Let everyone do the best he can for realising his own ideal.

Nor is it right that I should be judged by your standard or you by mine. The apple tree should not be judged by the standard of the oak, nor the oak by that of the apple. To judge the apple tree you must take the apple standard, and for the oak, its own standard.

The Dangers of Attachment

How can this be done? We see that the impression of any action, to which we attach ourselves, remains.

I may meet hundreds of persons during the day, and among them meet also one whom I love; and when I retire at night, I may try to think of all the faces I saw, but only that face comes before the mind — the face which I met perhaps only for one minute, and which I loved; all the others have vanished. My attachment to this particular person caused a deeper impression on my mind than all the other faces.

Physiologically the impressions have all been the same; every one of the faces that I saw pictured itself on the retina, and the brain took the pictures in, and yet there was no similarity of effect upon the mind. Most of the faces, perhaps, were entirely new faces, about which I had never thought before, but that one face of which I got only a glimpse found associations inside. Perhaps I had pictured him in my mind for years, knew hundreds of things about him, and this one new vision of him awakened hundreds of sleeping memories in my mind; and this one impression having been repeated perhaps a hundred times more than those of the different faces together, will produce a great effect on the mind.

Therefore, be "unattached"; let things work; let brain centres work; work incessantly, but let not a ripple conquer the mind. Work as if you were a stranger in this land, a sojourner; work incessantly, but do not bind yourselves; bondage is terrible. This world is not our habitation, it is only one of the many stages through which we are passing.

Remember that great saying of the Sankhya, "The whole of nature is for the soul, not the soul for nature." The very reason of nature's existence is for the education of the soul; it has no other meaning; it is there because the soul must have knowledge, and through knowledge free itself.

If we remember this always, we shall never be attached to nature; we shall know that nature is a book in which we are to read, and that when we have gained the required knowledge, the book is of no more value to us.

Instead of that, however, we are identifying ourselves with nature; we are thinking that the soul is for nature, that the spirit is for the flesh, and, as the common saying has it, we think that man "lives to eat" and not "eats to live". We are continually making this mistake; we are regarding nature as ourselves and are becoming attached to it; and as soon as this attachment comes, there is the deep impression on the soul, which binds us down and makes us work not from freedom but like slaves.

Learn to help without pitying or feeling that there is any misery. Learn to be the same to enemy and to friend; then when you can do that and no longer have any desire, the goal is attained.

Cut down the banyan tree of desire with the axe of non-attachment, and it will vanish utterly. It is all illusion. "He from whom blight and delusion have fallen, he who has conquered the evils of association, he alone is azad (free)."

To love anyone personally is bondage. Love all alike, then all desires fall off. Time, the "eater of everything", comes, and all has to go. Why try to improve the earth, to paint the butterfly? It all has to go at last. Do not be mere white mice in a treadmill, working always and never accomplishing anything. Every desire is fraught with evil, whether the desire itself be good or evil. It is like a dog jumping for a piece of meat which is ever receding from his reach, and dying a dog's death at last. Do not be like that. Cut off all desire.

By thinking about sense objects, attachment to them is formed. From attachment comes longing, and longing breeds anger.

From anger comes delusion, and from delusion, confused memory. From confused memory comes the ruin of discrimination; and from the ruin of discrimination, a man perishes.

There is then no peace in the heart of a carnal man, nor in him that is addicted to outward things, but in the spiritual and devout man.

The Vedanta philosophy says that this whole universe — mental, physical, moral — is hypnotic. Who is the cause of this hypnotism? You yourself are to blame. This weeping and wailing and knocking your heads into corners against brick walls, as it were, will not do you the least good.

However, knocking everything that is hypnotic on the head leads to what is called non-attachment; and clinging to more and more hypnotism is attachment. That is why in all religions you will find they wanted to give up the world, although many of them do not understand it.

There was a poor man who wanted some money; and somehow, he had heard that if he could get hold of a ghost, he might command him to bring money or anything else he liked; so he was very anxious to get hold of a ghost. At last he found a sage with great powers, and besought his help. The sage asked him what he would do with a ghost.

"I want a ghost to work for me; teach me how to get hold of one, sir; I desire it very much," replied the man.

But the sage said, "Don't disturb yourself, go home."

The next day the man went again to the sage and began to weep and pray, "Give me a ghost; I must have a ghost, sir, to help me."

At last the sage was disgusted, and said, "Take this charm, repeat this magic word, and a ghost will come, and whatever you say to him he will do. But beware; they are terrible beings, and must be kept continually busy. If you fail to give him work, he will take your life."

The man replied, "That is easy; I can give him work for all his life."

Then he went to a forest, and after long repetition of the magic word, a huge ghost appeared before him, and said, "I am a ghost. I have been conquered by your magic; but you must keep me constantly employed. The moment you fail to give me work I will kill you."

The man said, "Build me a palace," and the ghost said, "It is done; the palace is built."

"Bring me money," said the man. "Here is your money," said the ghost.

"Cut this forest down, and build a city in its place."

"That is done," said the ghost, "anything more?"

Now the man began to be frightened and thought he could give him nothing more to do; he did everything in a trice.

The ghost said, “Give me something to do or I will eat you up.”

The poor man could find no further occupation for him, and was frightened. So he ran and ran and at last reached the sage, and said, “Oh, sir, protect my life!”

The sage said, “I will find you a way out. Look at that dog with a curly tail. Draw your sword quickly and cut the tail off and give it to the ghost to straighten out.”

The man cut off the dog’s tail and gave it to the ghost, saying, “Straighten that out for me.”

The ghost took it and slowly and carefully straightened it out, but as soon as he let it go, it instantly curled up again. Once more he laboriously straightened it out, only to find it again curled up as soon as he attempted to let go of it. Again he patiently straightened it out, but as soon as he let it go, it curled up again.

So he went on for days and days, until he was exhausted and said, “I was never in such trouble before in my life. I am an old veteran ghost, but never before was I in such trouble. I will make a compromise with you,” he said to the man, “you let me off and I will let you keep all I have given you and will promise not to harm you.”

The man was much pleased, and accepted the offer gladly.

This world is like a dog's curly tail, and people have been striving to straighten it out for hundreds of years; but when they let it go, it has curled up again. How could it be otherwise? One must first know how to work without attachment, then one will not be a fanatic.

When we know that this world is like a dog's curly tail and will never get straightened, we shall not become fanatics. If there were no fanaticism in the world, it would make much more progress than it does now.

It is a mistake to think that fanaticism can make for the progress of mankind. On the contrary, it is a retarding element creating hatred and anger, and causing people to fight each other, and making them unsympathetic. We think that whatever we do or possess is the best in the world, and what we do not do or possess is of no value.

So, always remember the instance of the curly tail of the dog whenever you have a tendency to become a fanatic. You need not worry or make yourself sleepless about the world; it will go on without you.

When you have avoided fanaticism, then alone will you work well. It is the level-headed man, the calm man, of good judgment and cool nerves, of great sympathy and love, who does good work and so does good to himself. The fanatic is foolish and has no sympathy; he can never straighten the world, nor himself become pure and perfect.

Let us work without desire for name or fame or rule over others. Let us be free from the triple bonds of lust, greed of gain, and anger. And this truth is with us!

Was Krishna cunning? No, he was not cunning. He tried his best to prevent the war. It was Duryodhana who forced the war. But, when once in the thing, you should not recede — that is the man of duty. Do not run away, it is cowardice. When in the thing, you must do it. You should not budge an inch — of course not for a wrong thing; this war was a righteous war.

The devil comes in many guises — anger in the form of justice — passion in the form of duty. When it first comes, the man knows and then he forgets. Just as your pleaders' conscience; at first they know it is all Badmashi (roguery), then it is duty to their clients; at last they get hardened.

Leave off your commercial calculating ideas. If you can get rid of your attachment to a single thing, you are on the way to liberation.

Look at Krishna: he was great as a son, as a king, as a father, and all through his life he practiced the marvellous teachings which he preached."

"He who in the midst of the greatest activity finds the sweetest peace, and in the midst of the greatest calmness is most active, he has known the secret of life."

Krishna shows the way how to do this — by being non-attached: do everything but do not get identified with anything. You are the soul, the pure, the free, all the time; you are the Witness. Our misery comes, not from work, but by our getting attached to something.

Take for instance, money: money is a great thing to have, earn it, says Krishna; struggle hard to get money, but don't get attached to it. So with children, with wife, husband, relatives, fame, everything; you have no need to shun them, only don't get attached.

There is only one attachment and that belongs to the Lord, and to none other. Work for them, love them, do good to them, sacrifice a hundred lives, if need be, for them, but never be attached. His own life was the exact exemplification of that.

Attachment with Detachment

This whole universe is only one speck of the infinite being; and all our laws, our bondages, our joys and our sorrows, our happinesses and our expectations, are only within this small universe; all our progression and digression are within its small compass.

So you see how childish it is to expect a continuation of this universe — the creation of our minds — and to expect to go to heaven, which after all must mean only a repetition of this world that we know. You see at once that it is an impossible and childish desire to make the whole of infinite existence conform to the limited and conditioned existence which we know.

When a man says that he will have again and again this same thing which he is hating now, or, as I sometimes put it, when he asks for a comfortable religion, you may know that he has become so degenerate that he cannot think of anything higher than what he is now; he is just his little present surroundings and nothing more. He has forgotten his infinite nature, and his whole idea is confined to these little joys, and sorrows, and heart-jealousies of the moment.

He thinks that this finite thing is the infinite; and not only so, he will not let this foolishness go. He clings on desperately unto Trishna, and the thirst after life, what the Buddhists call Tanha and Tissa. There may be millions of kinds of happiness, and beings, and laws, and progress, and causation, all acting outside the little universe that we know; and, after all, the whole of this comprises but one section of our infinite nature.

To acquire freedom we have to get beyond the limitations of this universe; it cannot be found here. Perfect equilibrium, or what the Christians call the peace that passeth all understanding, cannot be had in this universe, nor in heaven, nor in any place where our mind and thoughts can go, where the senses can feel, or which the imagination can conceive.

No such place can give us that freedom, because all such places would be within our universe, and it is limited by space, time, and causation. There may be places that are more ethereal than this earth of ours, where enjoyments may be keener, but even those places must be in the universe and, therefore, in bondage to law; so we have to go beyond, and real religion begins where this little universe ends. These little joys, and sorrows, and knowledge of things end there, and the reality begins.

Until we give up the thirst after life, the strong attachment to this our transient conditioned existence we have no hope of catching even a glimpse of that infinite freedom beyond. It stands to reason then that there is only one way to attain to that freedom which is the goal of all the noblest aspirations of mankind, and that is by giving up this little life, giving up this little universe, giving up this earth, giving up heaven, giving up the body, giving up the mind, giving up everything that is limited and conditioned.

If we give up our attachment to this little universe of the senses or of the mind, we shall be free immediately. The only way to come out of bondage is to go beyond the limitations of law, to go beyond causation.

But it is a most difficult thing to give up the clinging to this universe; few ever attain to that. There are two ways to do that mentioned in our books. One is called the "Neti, Neti" (not this, not this), the other is called "Iti" (this); the former is the negative, and the latter is the positive way.

The negative way is the most difficult. It is only possible to the men of the very highest, exceptional minds and gigantic wills who simply stand up and say, "No, I will not have this," and the mind and body obey their will, and they come out successful.

But such people are very rare. The vast majority of mankind choose the positive way, the way through the world, making use of all the bondages themselves to break those very bondages. This is also a kind of giving up; only it is done slowly and gradually, by knowing things, enjoying things and thus obtaining experience, and knowing the nature of things until the mind lets them all go at last and becomes unattached.

The former way of obtaining non-attachment is by reasoning, and the latter way is through work and experience. The first is the path of Jnana-Yoga, and is characterized by the refusal to do any work; the second is that of Karma-Yoga, in which there is no cessation from work.

Every one must work in the universe. Only those who are perfectly satisfied with the Self, whose desires do not go beyond the Self, whose mind never strays out of the Self, to whom the Self is all in all, only those do not work. The rest must work.

A current rushing down of its own nature falls into a hollow and makes a whirlpool, and, after running a little in that whirlpool, it emerges again in the form of the free current to go on unchecked. Each human life is like that current. It gets into the whirl, gets involved in this world of space, time, and causation, whirls round a little, crying out, "my father, my brother, my name, my fame", and so on, and at last emerges out of it and regains its original freedom.

The whole universe is doing that. Whether we know it or not, whether we are conscious or unconscious of it, we are all working to get out of the dream of the world. Man's experience in the world is to enable him to get out of its whirlpool.

As children we all think that the world is made so very nice, and that masses of pleasures are simply waiting for our going out to them. That is every schoolboy's dream. And when he goes out into the world, the everyday world, very soon his dreams vanish. So with nations. When they see how every city is built upon ruins — every forest stands upon a city — then they become convinced of the vanity of this world.

All the power of knowledge and wealth once made has passed away — all the sciences of the ancients, lost, lost forever. Nobody knows how. That teaches us a grand lesson. Vanity of vanities; all is vanity and vexation of the spirit. If we have seen all this, then we become disgusted with this world and all it offers us. This is called Vairagya, non-attachment, and is the first step towards knowledge.

To attain this unattachment is almost a life-work, but as soon as we have reached this point, we have attained the goal of love and become free; the bondage of nature falls from us, and we see nature as she is; she forges no more chains for us; we stand entirely free and take not the results of work into consideration; who then cares for what the results may be?

Do you ask anything from your children in return for what you have given them? It is your duty to work for them, and there the matter ends. In whatever you do for a particular person, a city, or a state, assume the same attitude towards it as you have towards your children — expect nothing in return. If you can invariably take the position of a giver, in which everything given by you is a free offering to the world, without any thought of return, then will your work bring you no attachment. Attachment comes only where we expect a return.

If working like slaves results in selfishness and attachment, working as master of our own mind gives rise to the bliss of non-attachment.

We say that we cannot do good without at the same time doing some evil, or do evil without doing some good.

Knowing this, how can we work? There have, therefore, been sects in this world who have in an astoundingly preposterous way preached slow suicide as the only means to get out of the world, because if a man lives, he has to kill poor little animals and plants or do injury to something or some one. So according to them the only way out of the world is to die.

The Jains have preached this doctrine as their highest ideal. This teaching seems to be very logical. But the true solution is found in the Gita. It is the theory of non-attachment, to be attached to nothing while doing our work of life.

Know that you are separated entirely from the world, though you are in the world, and that whatever you may be doing in it, you are not doing that for your own sake. Any action that you do for yourself will bring its effect to bear upon you. If it is a good action, you will have to take the good effect, and if bad, you will have to take the bad effect; but any action that is not done for your own sake, whatever it be, will have no effect on you.

There is to be found a very expressive sentence in our scriptures embodying this idea: "Even if he kill the whole universe (or be himself killed), he is neither the killer nor the killed, when he knows that he is not acting for himself at all."

Therefore Karma-Yoga teaches, "Do not give up the world; live in the world, imbibe its influences as much as you can; but if it be for your own enjoyment's sake, work not at all."

Enjoyment should not be the goal. First kill your self and then take the whole world as yourself; as the old Christians used to say, "The old man must die." This old man is the selfish idea that the whole world is made for our enjoyment.

Foolish parents teach their children to pray, "O Lord, Thou hast created this sun for me and this moon for me," as if the Lord has had nothing else to do than to create everything for these babies.

Do not teach your children such nonsense. Then again, there are people who are foolish in another way: they teach us that all these animals were created for us to kill and eat, and that this universe is for the enjoyment of men. That is all foolishness.

A tiger may say, "Man was created for me," and pray, "O Lord, how wicked are these men who do not come and place themselves before me to be eaten; they are breaking Your law."

If the world is created for us, we are also created for the world. That this world is created for our enjoyment is the most wicked idea that holds us down. This world is not for our sake. Millions pass out of it every year; the world does not feel it; millions of others are supplied in their place. Just as much as the world is for us, so we also are for the world.

To work properly, therefore, you have first to give up the idea of attachment. Secondly, do not mix in the fray, hold yourself as a witness and go on working.

My master used to say, "Look upon your children as a nurse does." The nurse will take your baby and fondle it and play with it and behave towards it as gently as if it were her own child; but as soon as you give her notice to quit, she is ready to start off bag and baggage from the house. Everything in the shape of attachment is forgotten; it will not give the ordinary nurse the least pang to leave your children and take up other children.

Even so are you to be with all that you consider your own. You are the nurse, and if you believe in God, believe that all these things which you consider yours are really His. The greatest weakness often insinuates itself as the greatest good and strength. It is a weakness to think that any one is dependent on me, and that I can do good to another. This belief is the mother of all our attachment, and through this attachment comes all our pain.

We must inform our minds that no one in this universe depends upon us; not one beggar depends on our charity; not one soul on our kindness; not one living thing on our help. All are helped on by nature, and will be so helped even though millions of us were not here. The course of nature will not stop for such as you and me; it is, as already pointed out, only a blessed privilege to you and to me that we are allowed, in the way of helping others, to educate ourselves.

This is a great lesson to learn in life, and when we have learned it fully, we shall never be unhappy; we can go and mix without harm in society anywhere and everywhere. You may have wives and husbands, and regiments of servants, and kingdoms to govern; if only you act on the principle that the world is not for you and does not inevitably need you, they can do you no harm.

This very year some of your friends may have died. Is the world waiting without going on, for them to come again? Is its current stopped? No, it goes on. So drive out of your mind the idea that you have to do something for the world; the world does not require any help from you.

It is sheer nonsense on the part of any man to think that he is born to help the world; it is simply pride, it is selfishness insinuating itself in the form of virtue. When you have trained your mind and your nerves to realise this idea of the world's non-dependence on you or on anybody, there will then be no reaction in the form of pain resulting from work.

When you give something to a man and expect nothing — do not even expect the man to be grateful — his ingratitude will not tell upon you, because you never expected anything, never thought you had any right to anything in the way of a return. You gave him what he deserved; his own Karma got it for him; your Karma made you the carrier thereof.

Why should you be proud of having given away something? You are the porter that carried the money or other kind of gift, and the world deserved it by its own Karma. Where is then the reason for pride in you? There is nothing very great in what you give to the world.

When you have acquired the feeling of non-attachment, there will then be neither good nor evil for you. It is only selfishness that causes the difference between good and evil. It is a very hard thing to understand, but you will come to learn in time that nothing in the universe has power over you until you allow it to exercise such a power. Nothing has power over the Self of man, until the Self becomes a fool and loses independence.

So, by non-attachment, you overcome and deny the power of anything to act upon you. It is very easy to say that nothing has the right to act upon you until you allow it to do so; but what is the true sign of the man who really does not allow anything to work upon him, who is neither happy nor unhappy when acted upon by the external world? The sign is that good or ill fortune causes no change in his mind: in all conditions he continues to remain the same.

In Krishna we find ... two ideas stand supreme in his message: The first is the harmony of different ideas; the second is non-attachment. A man can attain to perfection, the highest goal, sitting on a throne, commanding armies, working out big plans for nations. In fact, Krishna's great sermon was preached on the battlefield.

Krishna saw plainly through the vanity of all the mummeries, mockeries, and ceremonials of the old priests; and yet he saw some good in them.

This was the great work of Krishna: to clear our eyes and make us look with broader vision upon humanity in its march upward and onward. His was the first heart that was large enough to see truth in all, his the first lips that uttered beautiful words for each and all.

This Krishna preceded Buddha by some thousand years. ... A great many people do not believe that he ever existed. Some believe that the worship of Krishna grew out of the old sun worship. There seem to be several Krishnas: one was mentioned in the Upanishads, another was king, another a general. All have been lumped into one Krishna.

It does not matter much. The fact is, some individual comes who is unique in spirituality. Then all sorts of legends are invented around him. But, all the Bibles and stories which come to be cast upon this one person have to be recast in the mould of his character. All the stories of the New Testament have to be modelled upon the accepted life and character of Christ. In all of the Indian stories about Buddha the one central note of that whole life is kept up — sacrifice for others.

No one can get anything unless he earns it. This is an eternal law. We may sometimes think it is not so, but in the long run we become convinced of it. A man may struggle all his life for riches; he may cheat thousands, but he finds at last that he did not deserve to become rich, and his life becomes a trouble and a nuisance to him.

We may go on accumulating things for our physical enjoyment, but only what we earn is really ours. A fool may buy all the books in the world, and they will be in his library; but he will be able to read only those that he deserves to; and this deserving is produced by Karma.

Our Karma determines what we deserve and what we can assimilate. We are responsible for what we are; and whatever we wish ourselves to be, we have the power to make ourselves. If what we are now has been the result of our own past actions, it certainly follows that whatever we wish to be in future can be produced by our present actions; so we have to know how to act.

Karma-Yoga explains this secret and teaches where and how to work, how to employ to the greatest advantage the largest part of our energies in the work that is before us. But with this secret we must take into consideration the great objection against work, namely that it causes pain.

All misery and pain come from attachment. I want to do work; I want to do good to a human being; and it is ninety to one that that human being whom I have helped will prove ungrateful and go against me; and the result to me is pain. Such things deter mankind from working; and it spoils a good portion of the work and energy of mankind, this fear of pain and misery.

Karma-Yoga teaches us how to work for work's sake, unattached, without caring who is helped, and what for. The Karma-Yogi works because it is his nature, because he feels that it is good for him to do so, and he has no object beyond that.

His position in this world is that of a giver, and he never cares to receive anything. He knows that he is giving, and does not ask for anything in return and, therefore, he eludes the grasp of misery. The grasp of pain, whenever it comes, is the result of the reaction of "attachment".

I have been asked many times how we can work if we do not have the passion which we generally feel for work. I also thought in that way years ago, but as I am growing older, getting more experience, I find it is not true. The less passion there is, the better we work. The calmer we are, the better for us, and the more the amount of work we can do.

When we let loose our feelings, we waste so much energy, shatter our nerves, disturb our minds, and accomplish very little work. The energy which ought to have gone out as work is spent as mere feeling, which counts for nothing. It is only when the mind is very calm and collected that the whole of its energy is spent in doing good work.

And if you read the lives of the great workers which the world has produced, you will find that they were wonderfully calm men. Nothing, as it were, could throw them off their balance.

That is why the man who becomes angry never does a great amount of work, and the man whom nothing can make angry accomplishes so much. The man who gives way to anger, or hatred, or any other passion, cannot work; he only breaks himself to pieces, and does nothing practical. It is the calm, forgiving, equable, well-balanced mind that does the greatest amount of work.

Do not identify yourself with anything. Hold your mind free. All this that you see, the pains and the miseries, are but the necessary conditions of this world; poverty and wealth and happiness are but momentary; they do not belong to our real nature at all. Our nature is far beyond misery and happiness, beyond every object of the senses, beyond the imagination; and yet we must go on working all the time. "Misery comes through attachment, not through work." As soon as we identify ourselves with the work we do, we feel miserable; but if we do not identify ourselves with it, we do not feel that misery.

If a beautiful picture belonging to another is burnt, a man does not generally become miserable; but when his own picture is burnt, how miserable he feels! Why? Both were beautiful pictures, perhaps copies of the same original; but in one case very much more misery is felt than in the other. It is because in one case he identifies himself with the picture, and not in the other.

This "I and mine" causes the whole misery. With the sense of possession comes selfishness, and selfishness brings on misery. Every act of selfishness or thought of selfishness makes us attached to something, and immediately we are made slaves.

Therefore Karma-Yoga tells us to enjoy the beauty of all the pictures in the world, but not to identify ourselves with any of them. Never say "mine". Whenever we say a thing is "mine", misery will immediately come.

We all understand that desires are wrong, but what is meant by giving up desires? How could life go on? It would be the same suicidal advice, killing the desire and the man too. The solution is this. Not that you should not have property, not that you should not have things which are necessary and things which are even luxuries.

Have all that you want, and more, only know the truth and realise it. Wealth does not belong to anybody. Have no idea of proprietorship, possessorship. You are nobody, nor am I, nor anyone else.

All belongs to the Lord, because the opening verse told us to put the Lord in everything. God is in the wealth that you enjoy. He is in the desire that rises in your mind. He is in the things you buy to satisfy your desire; He is in your beautiful attire, in your beautiful ornaments. This is the line of thought.

All will be metamorphosed as soon as you begin to see things in that light. If you put God in your every movement, in your conversation, in your form, in everything, the whole scene changes, and the world, instead of appearing as one of woe and misery, will become a heaven.

"The kingdom of heaven is within you," says Jesus; so says the Vedanta, and every great teacher. "He that hath eyes to see, let him see, and he that hath ears to hear, let him hear." The Vedanta proves that the truth for which we have been searching all this time is present, and was all the time with us.

In our ignorance, we thought we had lost it, and went about the world crying and weeping, struggling to find the truth, while all along it was dwelling in our own hearts. There alone can we find it.

If we understand the giving up of the world in its old, crude sense, then it would come to this: that we must not work, that we must be idle, sitting like lumps of earth, neither thinking nor doing anything, but must become fatalists, driven about by every circumstance, ordered about by the laws of nature, drifting from place to place.

That would be the result. But that is not what is meant. We must work. Ordinary mankind, driven everywhere by false desire, what do they know of work? The man propelled by his own feelings and his own senses, what does he know about work? He works, who is not propelled by his own desires, by any selfishness whatsoever. He works, who has no ulterior motive in view. He works, who has nothing to gain from work.

Here are the two ways of giving up all attachment. The one is for those who do not believe in God, or in any outside help. They are left to their own devices; they have simply to work with their own will, with the powers of their mind and discrimination, saying, "I must be non-attached".

For those who believe in God there is another way, which is much less difficult. They give up the fruits of work unto the Lord; they work and are never attached to the results.

Whatever they see, feel, hear, or do, is for Him. For whatever good work we may do, let us not claim any praise or benefit. It is the Lord's; give up the fruits unto Him.

Let us stand aside and think that we are only servants obeying the Lord, our Master, and that every impulse for action comes from Him every moment. Whatever thou worshippest, whatever thou perceivest, whatever thou doest, give up all unto Him and be at rest.

Give up all desire and be at peace. Have neither friends nor foes, and live alone. Thus shall we travel having neither friends nor foes, neither pleasure nor pain, neither desire nor jealousy, injuring no creatures, being the cause of injury to no creatures — from mountain to mountain, from village to village, preaching the name of the Lord. Seek no help from high or low, from above or below. Desire nothing — and look upon this vanishing panorama as a witness and let it pass.

Give up all argumentation and other distractions. Is there anything in dry intellectual jargon? It only throws the mind off its balance and disturbs it.

Control the organs of the senses and control the mind. Bear every misery without even knowing that you are miserable. Think of nothing but liberation.

Combine seriousness with childlike naïveté . Live in harmony with all. Give up all idea of egoism, and entertain no sectarian views. Useless wrangling is a great sin.

Give up forever the desire for name and fame and power.

"Give up," says the Veda, "give up." That is the one way, "Give up".न प्रजया धनेन त्यागेनैकेऽमृतत्वमानशुः — "Neither through wealth, nor through progeny, but by giving up alone that immortality is to be reached."

Give up the burden of all deeds to the Lord; give all, both good and bad. Do not keep the good and give only the bad. God helps those who do not help themselves.

Weakness is the one cause of suffering. We become miserable because we are weak. We lie, steal, kill, and commit other crimes, because we are weak. We suffer because we are weak. We die because we are weak. Where there is nothing to weaken us, there is no death nor sorrow. We are miserable through delusion. Give up the delusion, and the whole thing vanishes. It is plain and simple indeed. Through all these philosophical discussions and tremendous mental gymnastics we come to this one religious idea, the simplest in the whole world.

You remember that passage in the sermon of Buddha, how he sent a thought of love towards the south, the north, the east, and the west, above and below, until the whole universe was filled with this lose, so grand, great, and infinite. When you have that feeling, you have true personality. The whole universe is one person; let go the little things. Give up the small for the Infinite, give up small enjoyments for infinite bliss.

Most of the religions understand the fact, but the error into which they all seem to fall is the same; they are carried away by the heart, the feelings. There is evil in the world, give up the world; that is the great teaching, and the only teaching, no doubt.

Give up the world. There cannot be two opinions that to understand the truth everyone of us has to give up error. There cannot be two opinions that everyone of us in order to have good must give up evil; there cannot be two opinions that everyone of us to have life must give up what is death.

And yet, what remains to us, if this theory involves giving up the life of the senses, the life as we know it? And what else do we mean by life? If we give this up, what remains?

In Vedanta alone we find a rational solution of the problem. Here I can only lay before you what the Vedanta seeks to teach, and that is the deification of the world. The Vedanta does not in reality denounce the world. The ideal of renunciation nowhere attains such a height as in the teachings of the Vedanta.

But, at the same time, dry suicidal advice is not intended; it really means deification of the world — giving up the world as we think of it, as we know it, as it appears to us — and to know what it really is. Deify it; it is God alone. We read at the commencement of one of the oldest of the Upanishads, "Whatever exists in this universe is to be covered with the Lord."

We have to cover everything with the Lord Himself, not by a false sort of optimism, not by blinding our eyes to the evil, but by really seeing God in everything. Thus we have to give up the world, and when the world is given up, what remains? God.

Renunciation of the senses and desires is the only way out of this misery. If you want to be spiritual, you must renounce. This is the real test. Give up the world — this nonsense of the senses. There is only one real desire: to know what is true, to be spiritual. No more materialism, no more this egoism, I must become spiritual.

Strong, intense must be the desire. If a man's hands and feet were so tied that he could not move and then if a burning piece of charcoal were placed on his body, he would struggle with all his power to throw it off. When I shall have that sort of extreme desire, that restless struggle, to throw off this burning world, then the time will have come for me to glimpse the Divine Truth.

Give up this little life of yours. What matters it if you die of starvation — you and I and thousands like us — so long as this nation lives? What matters it if this little life goes? Everyone has to die, the saint or the sinner, the rich or the poor. The body never remains for anyone. Arise and awake and be perfectly sincere. Give up your passive attitude, gird your loins and stand up.

The fact being that the Lord is in us, we are He, the eternal subject, the real ego, never to be objectified, and that all this objectifying process is mere waste of time and talent. When the soul becomes aware of this, it gives up objectifying and falls back more and more upon the subjective.

This is the evolution, less and less in the body and more and more in the mind — man the highest form, meaning in Sanskrit manas , thought — the animal that thinks and not the animal that "senses" only. This is what in theology is called "renunciation". The formation of society, the institution of marriage, the love for children, our good works, morality, and ethics are all different forms of renunciation.

All our lives in every society are the subjection of the will, the thirst, the desire. This surrender of the will or the fictitious self — or the desire to jump out of ourselves, as it were — the struggle still to objectify the subject — is the one phenomenon in this world of which all societies and social forms are various modes and stages. Love is the easiest and smoothest way towards the self-surrender or subjection of the will and hatred, the opposite.

Karma-Yoga is purifying the mind by means of work. Now if any work is done, good or bad, it must produce as a result a good or bad effect; no power can stay it, once the cause is present.

Therefore good action producing good Karma, and bad action, bad Karma, the soul will go on in eternal bondage without ever hoping for deliverance. Now Karma belongs only to the body or the mind, never to the Atman (Self); only it can cast a veil before the Atman.

The veil cast by bad Karma is ignorance. Good Karma has the power to strengthen the moral powers. And thus it creates non-attachment; it destroys the tendency towards bad Karma and thereby purifies the mind. But if the work is done with the intention of enjoyment, it then produces only that very enjoyment and does not purify the mind or Chitta.

Therefore all work should be done without any desire to enjoy the fruits thereof. All fear and all desire to enjoy here or hereafter must be banished for ever by the Karma-Yogi. Moreover, this Karma without desire of return will destroy the selfishness, which is the root of all bondage.

The watchword of the Karma-Yogi is "not I, but Thou", and no amount of self-sacrifice is too much for him. But he does this without any desire to go to heaven, or gain name or fame or any other benefit in this world.

Although the explanation and rationale of this unselfish work is only in Jnana-Yoga, yet the natural divinity of man makes him love all sacrifice simply for the good of others, without any ulterior motive, whatever his creed or opinion. Again, with many the bondage of wealth is very great; and Karma-Yoga is absolutely necessary for them as breaking the crystallisation that has gathered round their love of money.

He is free, he is great, who turns his back upon the world, who has renounced everything, who has controlled his passion, and who thirsts for peace. One may gain political and social independence, but if one is a slave to his passions and desires, one cannot feel the pure joy of real freedom.

It is in the nature of work to be impelled ordinarily by motive and by attachment. In the presence of an ever active Providence who notes even the sparrow's fall, how can man attach any importance to his own work? Will it not be a blasphemy to do so when we know that He is taking care of the minutest things in the world?

We have only to stand in awe and reverence before Him saying, "Thy will be done". The highest men cannot work, for in them there is no attachment. Those whose whole soul is gone into the Self, those whose desires are confined in the Self, who have become ever associated with the Self, for them there is no work.

Such are indeed the highest of mankind; but apart from them every one else has to work. In so working we should never think that we can help on even the least thing in this universe. We cannot. We only help ourselves in this gymnasium of the world. This is the proper attitude of work. If we work in this way, if we always remember that our present opportunity to work thus is a privilege which has been given to us, we shall never be attached to anything.

Millions like you and me think that we are great people in the world; but we all die, and in five minutes the world forgets us. But the life of God is infinite. "Who can live a moment, breathe a moment, if this all-powerful One does not will it?"

He is the ever active Providence. All power is His and within His command. Through His command the winds blow, the sun shines, the earth lives, and death stalks upon the earth. He is the all in all; He is all and in all. We can only worship Him.

Give up all fruits of work; do good for its own sake; then alone will come perfect non-attachment. The bonds of the heart will thus break, and we shall reap perfect freedom. This freedom is indeed the goal of Karma-Yoga.

Discipline as an Ideal

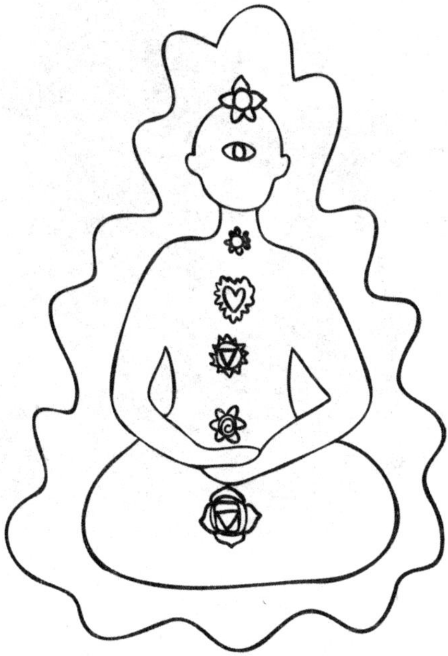

The Hindu Ideal of life is Nivarti; it means subjugation and conquest of evil passions, of nature of lust, revenge and avarice.

It does not mean conquest of all desire. It means only the annihilation of gross desires.

Every man is bound to love and sympathize with his fellow-creatures. A Sanyasi is one who has vanquished all his selfish passions and vowed to devote his life for the good of others. He loves all.

Sanyasis ought to be fed. They are not like the Christian bishops and Archbishops who must be paid to do their work with thousands of pounds per annum; all whose earnings are spent upon their own luxury — their wife and children.

The Sanyasi wants only a morsel of food, and then he places all his knowledge and services at the disposal of the public. He is a wandering missionary. Individuals and society have to work themselves up from "brute through man, into divine".

Even the lowest of the Hindus, the Pariah, has less of the brute in him than a Briton in a similar social status. This is the result of an old and excellent religious civilization. This evolution to a higher spiritual state is possible only through discipline and education.

Sometimes it is a good discipline to be forced to work for work's sake, even to the length of not being allowed to enjoy the fruits of one's labour.

Our motherland is a glowing example of the results and consequence of the eternal subjection of the individual to society and forced self-sacrifice by dint of institution and discipline.

In this country men are born according to Shastric injunctions, they eat and drink by prescribed rules throughout life, they go through marriage and kindred functions in the same way; in short, they even die according to Shastric injunctions. The hard discipline, with the exception of one great good point, is fraught with evil.

The good point is that men can do one or two things well with very little effort, having practiced them every day through generations. The delicious rice and curry which a cook of this country prepares with the aid of three lumps of earth and a few sticks can be had nowhere else. With the simple mechanism of an antediluvian loom, worth one rupee, and the feet put in a pit, it is possible to make kincobs worth twenty rupees a yard, in this country alone.

A torn mat, an earthen lamp, and that fed by castor oil — with the aid of materials such as these, wonderful savants are produced in this country alone. An all-forbearing attachment to an ugly and deformed wife, and a lifelong devotion to a worthless and villainous husband are possible in this country alone. Thus far the bright side.

But all these things are done by people guided like lifeless machines. There is no mental activity, no unfoldment of the heart, no vibration of life, no flux of hope; there is no strong stimulation of the will, no experience of keen pleasure, nor the contact of intense sorrow; there is no stir of inventive genius, no desire for novelty, no appreciation of new things.

Clouds never pass away from this mind; the radiant picture of the morning sun never charms this heart. It never even occurs to this mind if there is any better state than this; where it does, it cannot convince; in the event of conviction, effort is lacking; and even where there is effort, lack of enthusiasm kills it out.

If living by rule alone ensures excellence, if it be virtue to follow strictly the rules and customs handed down through generations, say then, who is more virtuous than a tree, who is a greater devotee, a holier saint, than a railway train? Who has ever seen a piece of stone transgress a natural law? Who has ever known cattle to commit sin?

Again, can that be called society which is formed by an aggregate of men who are like lumps of clay, like lifeless machines, like heaped up pebbles? How can such society fare well? Were good possible, then instead of being slaves for hundreds of years, we would have been the greatest nation on earth, and this soil of India, instead of being a mine of stupidity, would have been the eternal fountain-head of learning.

Temporal Enjoyments

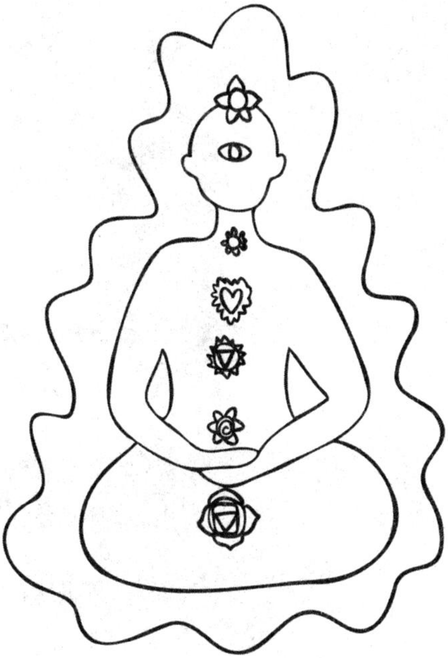

Whatever work we do, the mind is thrown into a wave, and after the work is finished, we think the wave is gone. No. It has only become fine, but it is still there. When we try to remember the work, it comes up again and becomes a wave. So it was there; if not, there would not have been memory.

Thus every action, every thought, good or bad, just goes down and becomes fine, and is there stored up. Both happy and unhappy thoughts are called pain-bearing obstructions, because according to the Yogis, they, in the long run, bring pain.

All happiness which comes from the senses will, eventually, bring pain. All enjoyment will make us thirst for more, and that brings pain as its result. There is no limit to man's desires; he goes on desiring, and when he comes to a point where desire cannot be fulfilled, the result is pain.

Therefore the Yogis regard the sum-total of the impressions, good or evil, as pain-bearing obstructions; they obstruct the way to freedom of the Soul.

The first ideal of the attempt to realise religion is that of renunciation. As far as we can, we must give up. Darkness and light, enjoyment of the world and enjoyment of God will never go together. "Ye cannot serve God and Mammon." Let people try it if they will, and I have seen millions in every country who have tried; but after all, it comes to nothing. If one word remains true in the saying, it is, give up everything for the sake of the Lord. This is a hard and long task, but you can begin it here and now. Bit by bit we must go towards it.

The goal of man is to go beyond law. And enjoyment can never be the goal, because enjoyment can only be in nature. Alas, alas, the desire for enjoyment does not leave a man.

Enjoyment, misery, luxury, wealth, power, and poverty, even life itself, are all evanescent.

Everything that has selfishness for its basis, competition as its right hand, and enjoyment as its goal, must die sooner or later. Such things must die.

Enjoyment is the million-headed serpent that we must tread under foot. We renounce and go on, then find nothing and despair; but hold on, hold on . The world is a demon. It is a kingdom of which the puny ego is king.

Put it away and stand firm. Give up lust and gold and fame and hold fast to the Lord, and at last we shall reach a state of perfect indifference. The idea that the gratification of the senses constitutes enjoyment is purely materialistic. There is not one spark of real enjoyment there; all the joy there is, is a mere reflection of the true bliss.

Plunder and fight as you may, the enjoyment that you are seeking is only in peace; and peace, in the renunciation of physical pleasures. Enjoyment lies not in physical development, but in the culture of the mind and the intellect.

Is enjoyment the goal of life? Were it so, it would be a tremendous mistake to become a man at all. What man can enjoy a meal with more gusto than the dog or the cat ? Go to a menagerie and see the wild animals tearing the flesh from the bone. Go back and become a bird! What a mistake then to become a man! Vain have been my years — hundreds of years — of struggle only to become the man of sense-enjoyments.

What is the goal of it all? Can senses ever be the goal? Can enjoyment of pleasure ever be the goal? Can this life ever be the goal of the soul? If it is, better die this moment; do not want this life! If that is the fate of man, that he is going to be only the perfected machine, it would just mean that we go back to being trees and stones and things like that.

Did you ever hear a cow tell a lie or see a tree steal? They are perfect machines. They do not make mistakes. They live in a world where everything is finished.

So long as enjoyment is sought, bondage remains. Only imperfection can enjoy, because enjoyment is the fulfilling of desire. The human soul enjoys nature. The underlying reality of nature, soul, and God is Brahman; but It (Brahman) is unseen, until we bring It out.

It may be brought out by Pramantha or friction, just as we can produce fire by friction. The body is the lower piece of wood, Om is the pointed piece and Dhyana (meditation) is the friction. When this is used, that light which is the knowledge of Brahman will burst forth in the soul.

The lower the animal, the more is its enjoyment in the senses, the more it lives in the senses. Civilisation, true civilization, should mean the power of taking the animal-man out of his sense-life — by giving him visions and tastes of planes much higher — and not external comforts.

Man knows this instinctively. He may not formulate it to himself under all circumstances. He may form very divergent opinions about the life of thought. But it is there, pressing itself to the front in spite of everything, making him pay reverence to the hoodoo-worker, the medicine-man, the magician, the priest, or the professor of science.

The growth of man can only be gauged by his power of living in the higher atmosphere where the senses are left behind, the amount of the pure thought-oxygen his lungs can breathe in, and the amount of time he can spend on that height.

As it is, it is an obvious fact that, with the exception of what is taken up by the necessities of life, the man of culture is loth to spend his time on so-called comforts, and even necessary actions are performed with lessened zeal, as the process moves forward.

The other great mistake we often make is that good is taken as an ever-increasing item, whilst evil is a fixed quantity. From this it is argued that evil being diminished every day, there will come a time when good alone will remain.

The fallacy lies in the assumption of a false premise. If good is increasing, so is evil. My desires have been much more than the desires of the masses among my race. My joys have been much greater than theirs — but my miseries a million times more intense. The same constitution that makes you feel the least touch of good makes you feel the least of evil too. The same nerves that carry sensations of pleasure carry the sensations of pain too — and the same mind feels both.

The progress of the world means more enjoyment and more misery too. This mixture of life and death, good and evil, knowledge and ignorance is what is called Maya — or the universal phenomenon.

You may go on for eternity inside this net, seeking for happiness — you find much, and much evil too. To have good and no evil is childish nonsense.

Two ways are left open — one by giving up all hope to take up the world as it is and bear the pangs and pains in the hope of a crumb of happiness now and then. The other, to give up the search for pleasure, knowing it to be pain in another form, and seek for truth — and those that dare try for truth succeed in finding that truth as ever present — present in themselves.

Then we also discover how the same truth is manifesting itself both in our relative error and knowledge — we find also that the same truth is bliss which again is manifesting itself as good and evil, and with it also we find real existence which is manifesting itself as both death and life.

Nowadays people among the backward nations, and among the less cultured portion of the civilised people of the West are laying much stress on the non-essential. Among the cultured and the wealthy, matters are on a different footing. The wealthy are either immersed in the enjoyment of health or grubbing for more. They, and a large section of the busy people, say of religion that it is rot, stuff, nonsense, and they honestly think so.

There never was a person who found happiness in the senses or in enjoyment of the senses. The world is our fish basket, we must not depend upon it for enjoyment. This is a place for action, not enjoyment.

Through enjoyment Yoga will come in time. But alas, such is the lot of my countrymen that, not to speak of possessing yoga, they cannot even have a little Bhoga! Suffering all sorts of indignities they can with the utmost difficulty only meet the barest needs of the body—and even that everyone cannot do! It is strange that such a state of affairs does not disturb our sleep and rouse us to our immediate duties.

To the vast majority of mankind, the body is everything; the body is all the universe to them; bodily enjoyment is their all in all. This demon of the worship of the body and of the things of the body has entered into us all. We may indulge in tall talk and take very high flights, but we are like vultures all the same; our mind is directed to the piece of carrion down below.

Why should our body be saved, say, from the tiger? Why may we not give it over to the tiger? The tiger will thereby be pleased, and that is not altogether so very far from self-sacrifice and worship.

Can you reach the realization of such an idea in which all sense of self is completely lost? It is a very dizzy height on the pinnacle of the religion of love, and few in this world have ever climbed up to it; but until a man reaches that highest point of ever-ready and ever-willing self-sacrifice, he cannot become a perfect Bhakta.

We may all manage to maintain our bodies more or less satisfactorily and for longer or shorter intervals of time. Nevertheless, our bodies have to go; there is no permanence about them. Blessed are they whose bodies get destroyed in the service of others.

“Wealth, and even life itself, the sage always holds ready for the service of others. In this world, there being one thing certain, viz death, it is far better that this body dies in a good cause than in a bad one.”

We may drag our life on for fifty years or a hundred years; but after that, what is it that happens? Everything that is the result of combination must get dissolved and die. There must and will come a time for it to be decomposed. Jesus and Buddha and Mohammed are all dead; all the great Prophets and Teachers of the world are dead.

The history of the world shows that evil is a continuously increasing quantity, as well as good. Take the lowest man; he lives in the forest. His sense of enjoyment is very small, and so also is his power to suffer.

His misery is entirely on the sense-plane. If he does not get plenty of food, he is miserable; but give him plenty of food and freedom to rove and to hunt, and he is perfectly happy. His happiness consists only in the senses, and so does his misery also.

But if that man increases in knowledge, his happiness will increase, the intellect will open to him, and his sense-enjoyment will evolve into intellectual enjoyment. He will feel pleasure in reading a beautiful poem, and a mathematical problem will be of absorbing interest to him. But, with these, the inner nerves will become more and more susceptible to miseries of mental pain, of which the savage does not think.

Take a very simple illustration. In Tibet there is no marriage, and there is no jealousy, yet we know that marriage is a much higher state. The Tibetans have not known the wonderful enjoyment, the blessing of chastity, the happiness of having a chaste, virtuous wife, or a chaste, virtuous husband. These people cannot feel that.

And similarly they do not feel the intense jealousy of the chaste wife or husband, or the misery caused by unfaithfulness on either side, with all the heart-burnings and sorrows which believers in chastity experience. On one side, the latter gain happiness, but on the other, they suffer misery too.

This whole universe is only one speck of the infinite being; and all our laws, our bondages, our joys and our sorrows, our happinesses and our expectations, are only within this small universe; all our progression and digression are within its small compass.

So you see how childish it is to expect a continuation of this universe — the creation of our minds — and to expect to go to heaven, which after all must mean only a repetition of this world that we know. You see at once that it is an impossible and childish desire to make the whole of infinite existence conform to the limited and conditioned existence which we know.

When a man says that he will have again and again this same thing which he is hating now, or, as I sometimes put it, when he asks for a comfortable religion, you may know that he has become so degenerate that he cannot think of anything higher than what he is now; he is just his little present surroundings and nothing more. He has forgotten his infinite nature, and his whole idea is confined to these little joys, and sorrows, and heart-jealousies of the moment.

He thinks that this finite thing is the infinite; and not only so, he will not let this foolishness go. He clings on desperately unto Trishna, and the thirst after life, what the Buddhists call Tanha and Tissa. There may be millions of kinds of happiness, and beings, and laws, and progress, and causation, all acting outside the little universe that we know; and, after all, the whole of this comprises but one section of our infinite nature.

To acquire freedom we have to get beyond the limitations of this universe; it cannot be found here. Perfect equilibrium, or what the Christians call the peace that passeth all understanding, cannot be had in this universe, nor in heaven, nor in any place where our mind and thoughts can go, where the senses can feel, or which the imagination can conceive.

No such place can give us that freedom, because all such places would be within our universe, and it is limited by space, time, and causation. There may be places that are more ethereal than this earth of ours, where enjoyments may be keener, but even those places must be in the universe and, therefore, in bondage to law; so we have to go beyond, and real religion begins where this little universe ends. These little joys, and sorrows, and knowledge of things end there, and the reality begins.

Until we give up the thirst after life, the strong attachment to this our transient conditioned existence we have no hope of catching even a glimpse of that infinite freedom beyond. It stands to reason then that there is only one way to attain to that freedom which is the goal of all the noblest aspirations of mankind, and that is by giving up this little life, giving up this little universe, giving up this earth, giving up heaven, giving up the body, giving up the mind, giving up everything that is limited and conditioned.

If we give up our attachment to this little universe of the senses or of the mind, we shall be free immediately. The only way to come out of bondage is to go beyond the limitations of law, to go beyond causation.

But it is a most difficult thing to give up the clinging to this universe; few ever attain to that. There are two ways to do that mentioned in our books. One is called the "Neti, Neti" (not this, not this), the other is called "Iti" (this); the former is the negative, and the latter is the positive way.

The negative way is the most difficult. It is only possible to the men of the very highest, exceptional minds and gigantic wills who simply stand up and say, "No, I will not have this," and the mind and body obey their will, and they come out successful.

But such people are very rare. The vast majority of mankind choose the positive way, the way through the world, making use of all the bondages themselves to break those very bondages. This is also a kind of giving up; only it is done slowly and gradually, by knowing things, enjoying things and thus obtaining experience, and knowing the nature of things until the mind lets them all go at last and becomes unattached.

The former way of obtaining non-attachment is by reasoning, and the latter way is through work and experience. The first is the path of Jnana-Yoga, and is characterized by the refusal to do any work; the second is that of Karma-Yoga, in which there is no cessation from work.

Every one must work in the universe. Only those who are perfectly satisfied with the Self, whose desires do not go beyond the Self, whose mind never strays out of the Self, to whom the Self is all in all, only those do not work. The rest must work.

A current rushing down of its own nature falls into a hollow and makes a whirlpool, and, after running a little in that whirlpool, it emerges again in the form of the free current to go on unchecked. Each human life is like that current. It gets into the whirl, gets involved in this world of space, time, and causation, whirls round a little, crying out, "my father, my brother, my name, my fame", and so on, and at last emerges out of it and regains its original freedom.

The whole universe is doing that. Whether we know it or not, whether we are conscious or unconscious of it, we are all working to get out of the dream of the world. Man's experience in the world is to enable him to get out of its whirlpool.

As children we all think that the world is made so very nice, and that masses of pleasures are simply waiting for our going out to them. That is every schoolboy's dream. And when he goes out into the world, the everyday world, very soon his dreams vanish. So with nations. When they see how every city is built upon ruins — every forest stands upon a city — then they become convinced of the vanity of this world.

All the power of knowledge and wealth once made has passed away — all the sciences of the ancients, lost, lost forever. Nobody knows how. That teaches us a grand lesson. Vanity of vanities; all is vanity and vexation of the spirit. If we have seen all this, then we become disgusted with this world and all it offers us. This is called Vairagya, non-attachment, and is the first step towards knowledge.

To attain this unattachment is almost a life-work, but as soon as we have reached this point, we have attained the goal of love and become free; the bondage of nature falls from us, and we see nature as she is; she forges no more chains for us; we stand entirely free and take not the results of work into consideration; who then cares for what the results may be?

Do you ask anything from your children in return for what you have given them? It is your duty to work for them, and there the matter ends. In whatever you do for a particular person, a city, or a state, assume the same attitude towards it as you have towards your children — expect nothing in return. If you can invariably take the position of a giver, in which everything given by you is a free offering to the world, without any thought of return, then will your work bring you no attachment. Attachment comes only where we expect a return.

If working like slaves results in selfishness and attachment, working as master of our own mind gives rise to the bliss of non-attachment.

We say that we cannot do good without at the same time doing some evil, or do evil without doing some good.

Knowing this, how can we work? There have, therefore, been sects in this world who have in an astoundingly preposterous way preached slow suicide as the only means to get out of the world, because if a man lives, he has to kill poor little animals and plants or do injury to something or some one. So according to them the only way out of the world is to die.

The Jains have preached this doctrine as their highest ideal. This teaching seems to be very logical. But the true solution is found in the Gita. It is the theory of non-attachment, to be attached to nothing while doing our work of life.

Know that you are separated entirely from the world, though you are in the world, and that whatever you may be doing in it, you are not doing that for your own sake. Any action that you do for yourself will bring its effect to bear upon you. If it is a good action, you will have to take the good effect, and if bad, you will have to take the bad effect; but any action that is not done for your own sake, whatever it be, will have no effect on you.

There is to be found a very expressive sentence in our scriptures embodying this idea: "Even if he kill the whole universe (or be himself killed), he is neither the killer nor the killed, when he knows that he is not acting for himself at all."

Therefore Karma-Yoga teaches, "Do not give up the world; live in the world, imbibe its influences as much as you can; but if it be for your own enjoyment's sake, work not at all."

Enjoyment should not be the goal. First kill your self and then take the whole world as yourself; as the old Christians used to say, "The old man must die." This old man is the selfish idea that the whole world is made for our enjoyment.

Foolish parents teach their children to pray, "O Lord, Thou hast created this sun for me and this moon for me," as if the Lord has had nothing else to do than to create everything for these babies.

Do not teach your children such nonsense. Then again, there are people who are foolish in another way: they teach us that all these animals were created for us to kill and eat, and that this universe is for the enjoyment of men. That is all foolishness.

A tiger may say, "Man was created for me," and pray, "O Lord, how wicked are these men who do not come and place themselves before me to be eaten; they are breaking Your law."

If the world is created for us, we are also created for the world. That this world is created for our enjoyment is the most wicked idea that holds us down. This world is not for our sake. Millions pass out of it every year; the world does not feel it; millions of others are supplied in their place. Just as much as the world is for us, so we also are for the world.

To work properly, therefore, you have first to give up the idea of attachment. Secondly, do not mix in the fray, hold yourself as a witness and go on working.

My master used to say, "Look upon your children as a nurse does." The nurse will take your baby and fondle it and play with it and behave towards it as gently as if it were her own child; but as soon as you give her notice to quit, she is ready to start off bag and baggage from the house. Everything in the shape of attachment is forgotten; it will not give the ordinary nurse the least pang to leave your children and take up other children.

Even so are you to be with all that you consider your own. You are the nurse, and if you believe in God, believe that all these things which you consider yours are really His. The greatest weakness often insinuates itself as the greatest good and strength. It is a weakness to think that any one is dependent on me, and that I can do good to another. This belief is the mother of all our attachment, and through this attachment comes all our pain.

We must inform our minds that no one in this universe depends upon us; not one beggar depends on our charity; not one soul on our kindness; not one living thing on our help. All are helped on by nature, and will be so helped even though millions of us were not here. The course of nature will not stop for such as you and me; it is, as already pointed out, only a blessed privilege to you and to me that we are allowed, in the way of helping others, to educate ourselves.

This is a great lesson to learn in life, and when we have learned it fully, we shall never be unhappy; we can go and mix without harm in society anywhere and everywhere. You may have wives and husbands, and regiments of servants, and kingdoms to govern; if only you act on the principle that the world is not for you and does not inevitably need you, they can do you no harm.

This very year some of your friends may have died. Is the world waiting without going on, for them to come again? Is its current stopped? No, it goes on. So drive out of your mind the idea that you have to do something for the world; the world does not require any help from you.

It is sheer nonsense on the part of any man to think that he is born to help the world; it is simply pride, it is selfishness insinuating itself in the form of virtue. When you have trained your mind and your nerves to realise this idea of the world's non-dependence on you or on anybody, there will then be no reaction in the form of pain resulting from work.

When you give something to a man and expect nothing — do not even expect the man to be grateful — his ingratitude will not tell upon you, because you never expected anything, never thought you had any right to anything in the way of a return. You gave him what he deserved; his own Karma got it for him; your Karma made you the carrier thereof.

\Why should you be proud of having given away something? You are the porter that carried the money or other kind of gift, and the world deserved it by its own Karma. Where is then the reason for pride in you? There is nothing very great in what you give to the world.

When you have acquired the feeling of non-attachment, there will then be neither good nor evil for you. It is only selfishness that causes the difference between good and evil. It is a very hard thing to understand, but you will come to learn in time that nothing in the universe has power over you until you allow it to exercise such a power. Nothing has power over the Self of man, until the Self becomes a fool and loses independence.

So, by non-attachment, you overcome and deny the power of anything to act upon you. It is very easy to say that nothing has the right to act upon you until you allow it to do so; but what is the true sign of the man who really does not allow anything to work upon him, who is neither happy nor unhappy when acted upon by the external world? The sign is that good or ill fortune causes no change in his mind: in all conditions he continues to remain the same.

In Krishna we find ... two ideas stand supreme in his message: The first is the harmony of different ideas; the second is non-attachment. A man can attain to perfection, the highest goal, sitting on a throne, commanding armies, working out big plans for nations. In fact, Krishna's great sermon was preached on the battlefield.

Krishna saw plainly through the vanity of all the mummeries, mockeries, and ceremonials of the old priests; and yet he saw some good in them.

This was the great work of Krishna: to clear our eyes and make us look with broader vision upon humanity in its march upward and onward. His was the first heart that was large enough to see truth in all, his the first lips that uttered beautiful words for each and all.

This Krishna preceded Buddha by some thousand years. ... A great many people do not believe that he ever existed. Some believe that the worship of Krishna grew out of the old sun worship. There seem to be several Krishnas: one was mentioned in the Upanishads, another was king, another a general. All have been lumped into one Krishna.

It does not matter much. The fact is, some individual comes who is unique in spirituality. Then all sorts of legends are invented around him. But, all the Bibles and stories which come to be cast upon this one person have to be recast in the mould of his character. All the stories of the New Testament have to be modelled upon the accepted life and character of Christ. In all of the Indian stories about Buddha the one central note of that whole life is kept up — sacrifice for others.

No one can get anything unless he earns it. This is an eternal law. We may sometimes think it is not so, but in the long run we become convinced of it. A man may struggle all his life for riches; he may cheat thousands, but he finds at last that he did not deserve to become rich, and his life becomes a trouble and a nuisance to him.

We may go on accumulating things for our physical enjoyment, but only what we earn is really ours. A fool may buy all the books in the world, and they will be in his library; but he will be able to read only those that he deserves to; and this deserving is produced by Karma.

Our Karma determines what we deserve and what we can assimilate. We are responsible for what we are; and whatever we wish ourselves to be, we have the power to make ourselves. If what we are now has been the result of our own past actions, it certainly follows that whatever we wish to be in future can be produced by our present actions; so we have to know how to act.

Karma-Yoga explains this secret and teaches where and how to work, how to employ to the greatest advantage the largest part of our energies in the work that is before us. But with this secret we must take into consideration the great objection against work, namely that it causes pain.

All misery and pain come from attachment. I want to do work; I want to do good to a human being; and it is ninety to one that that human being whom I have helped will prove ungrateful and go against me; and the result to me is pain. Such things deter mankind from working; and it spoils a good portion of the work and energy of mankind, this fear of pain and misery.

Karma-Yoga teaches us how to work for work's sake, unattached, without caring who is helped, and what for. The Karma-Yogi works because it is his nature, because he feels that it is good for him to do so, and he has no object beyond that.

His position in this world is that of a giver, and he never cares to receive anything. He knows that he is giving, and does not ask for anything in return and, therefore, he eludes the grasp of misery. The grasp of pain, whenever it comes, is the result of the reaction of "attachment".

I have been asked many times how we can work if we do not have the passion which we generally feel for work. I also thought in that way years ago, but as I am growing older, getting more experience, I find it is not true. The less passion there is, the better we work. The calmer we are, the better for us, and the more the amount of work we can do.

When we let loose our feelings, we waste so much energy, shatter our nerves, disturb our minds, and accomplish very little work. The energy which ought to have gone out as work is spent as mere feeling, which counts for nothing. It is only when the mind is very calm and collected that the whole of its energy is spent in doing good work.

And if you read the lives of the great workers which the world has produced, you will find that they were wonderfully calm men. Nothing, as it were, could throw them off their balance.

That is why the man who becomes angry never does a great amount of work, and the man whom nothing can make angry accomplishes so much. The man who gives way to anger, or hatred, or any other passion, cannot work; he only breaks himself to pieces, and does nothing practical. It is the calm, forgiving, equable, well-balanced mind that does the greatest amount of work.

Do not identify yourself with anything. Hold your mind free. All this that you see, the pains and the miseries, are but the necessary conditions of this world; poverty and wealth and happiness are but momentary; they do not belong to our real nature at all. Our nature is far beyond misery and happiness, beyond every object of the senses, beyond the imagination; and yet we must go on working all the time. "Misery comes through attachment, not through work." As soon as we identify ourselves with the work we do, we feel miserable; but if we do not identify ourselves with it, we do not feel that misery.

If a beautiful picture belonging to another is burnt, a man does not generally become miserable; but when his own picture is burnt, how miserable he feels! Why? Both were beautiful pictures, perhaps copies of the same original; but in one case very much more misery is felt than in the other. It is because in one case he identifies himself with the picture, and not in the other.

This "I and mine" causes the whole misery. With the sense of possession comes selfishness, and selfishness brings on misery. Every act of selfishness or thought of selfishness makes us attached to something, and immediately we are made slaves.

Therefore Karma-Yoga tells us to enjoy the beauty of all the pictures in the world, but not to identify ourselves with any of them. Never say "mine". Whenever we say a thing is "mine", misery will immediately come.

We all understand that desires are wrong, but what is meant by giving up desires? How could life go on? It would be the same suicidal advice, killing the desire and the man too. The solution is this. Not that you should not have property, not that you should not have things which are necessary and things which are even luxuries.

Have all that you want, and more, only know the truth and realise it. Wealth does not belong to anybody. Have no idea of proprietorship, possessorship. You are nobody, nor am I, nor anyone else.

All belongs to the Lord, because the opening verse told us to put the Lord in everything. God is in the wealth that you enjoy. He is in the desire that rises in your mind. He is in the things you buy to satisfy your desire; He is in your beautiful attire, in your beautiful ornaments. This is the line of thought.

All will be metamorphosed as soon as you begin to see things in that light. If you put God in your every movement, in your conversation, in your form, in everything, the whole scene changes, and the world, instead of appearing as one of woe and misery, will become a heaven.

"The kingdom of heaven is within you," says Jesus; so says the Vedanta, and every great teacher. "He that hath eyes to see, let him see, and he that hath ears to hear, let him hear." The Vedanta proves that the truth for which we have been searching all this time is present, and was all the time with us.

In our ignorance, we thought we had lost it, and went about the world crying and weeping, struggling to find the truth, while all along it was dwelling in our own hearts. There alone can we find it.

If we understand the giving up of the world in its old, crude sense, then it would come to this: that we must not work, that we must be idle, sitting like lumps of earth, neither thinking nor doing anything, but must become fatalists, driven about by every circumstance, ordered about by the laws of nature, drifting from place to place.

That would be the result. But that is not what is meant. We must work. Ordinary mankind, driven everywhere by false desire, what do they know of work? The man propelled by his own feelings and his own senses, what does he know about work? He works, who is not propelled by his own desires, by any selfishness whatsoever. He works, who has no ulterior motive in view. He works, who has nothing to gain from work.

Here are the two ways of giving up all attachment. The one is for those who do not believe in God, or in any outside help. They are left to their own devices; they have simply to work with their own will, with the powers of their mind and discrimination, saying, "I must be non-attached".

For those who believe in God there is another way, which is much less difficult. They give up the fruits of work unto the Lord; they work and are never attached to the results.

Whatever they see, feel, hear, or do, is for Him. For whatever good work we may do, let us not claim any praise or benefit. It is the Lord's; give up the fruits unto Him.

Let us stand aside and think that we are only servants obeying the Lord, our Master, and that every impulse for action comes from Him every moment. Whatever thou worshippest, whatever thou perceivest, whatever thou doest, give up all unto Him and be at rest.

Give up all desire and be at peace. Have neither friends nor foes, and live alone. Thus shall we travel having neither friends nor foes, neither pleasure nor pain, neither desire nor jealousy, injuring no creatures, being the cause of injury to no creatures — from mountain to mountain, from village to village, preaching the name of the Lord. Seek no help from high or low, from above or below. Desire nothing — and look upon this vanishing panorama as a witness and let it pass.

Give up all argumentation and other distractions. Is there anything in dry intellectual jargon? It only throws the mind off its balance and disturbs it.

Control the organs of the senses and control the mind. Bear every misery without even knowing that you are miserable. Think of nothing but liberation.

Combine seriousness with childlike naïveté . Live in harmony with all. Give up all idea of egoism, and entertain no sectarian views. Useless wrangling is a great sin.

Give up forever the desire for name and fame and power.

"Give up," says the Veda, "give up." That is the one way, "Give up". न प्रजया धनेन त्यागेनैकेऽमृतत्वमानशुः — "Neither through wealth, nor through progeny, but by giving up alone that immortality is to be reached."

Give up the burden of all deeds to the Lord; give all, both good and bad. Do not keep the good and give only the bad. God helps those who do not help themselves.

Weakness is the one cause of suffering. We become miserable because we are weak. We lie, steal, kill, and commit other crimes, because we are weak. We suffer because we are weak. We die because we are weak. Where there is nothing to weaken us, there is no death nor sorrow. We are miserable through delusion. Give up the delusion, and the whole thing vanishes. It is plain and simple indeed. Through all these philosophical discussions and tremendous mental gymnastics we come to this one religious idea, the simplest in the whole world.

You remember that passage in the sermon of Buddha, how he sent a thought of love towards the south, the north, the east, and the west, above and below, until the whole universe was filled with this lose, so grand, great, and infinite. When you have that feeling, you have true personality. The whole universe is one person; let go the little things. Give up the small for the Infinite, give up small enjoyments for infinite bliss.

Most of the religions understand the fact, but the error into which they all seem to fall is the same; they are carried away by the heart, the feelings. There is evil in the world, give up the world; that is the great teaching, and the only teaching, no doubt.

Give up the world. There cannot be two opinions that to understand the truth everyone of us has to give up error. There cannot be two opinions that everyone of us in order to have good must give up evil; there cannot be two opinions that everyone of us to have life must give up what is death.

And yet, what remains to us, if this theory involves giving up the life of the senses, the life as we know it? And what else do we mean by life? If we give this up, what remains?

In Vedanta alone we find a rational solution of the problem. Here I can only lay before you what the Vedanta seeks to teach, and that is the deification of the world. The Vedanta does not in reality denounce the world. The ideal of renunciation nowhere attains such a height as in the teachings of the Vedanta.

But, at the same time, dry suicidal advice is not intended; it really means deification of the world — giving up the world as we think of it, as we know it, as it appears to us — and to know what it really is. Deify it; it is God alone. We read at the commencement of one of the oldest of the Upanishads, "Whatever exists in this universe is to be covered with the Lord."

We have to cover everything with the Lord Himself, not by a false sort of optimism, not by blinding our eyes to the evil, but by really seeing God in everything. Thus we have to give up the world, and when the world is given up, what remains? God.

Renunciation of the senses and desires is the only way out of this misery. If you want to be spiritual, you must renounce. This is the real test. Give up the world — this nonsense of the senses. There is only one real desire: to know what is true, to be spiritual. No more materialism, no more this egoism, I must become spiritual.

Strong, intense must be the desire. If a man's hands and feet were so tied that he could not move and then if a burning piece of charcoal were placed on his body, he would struggle with all his power to throw it off. When I shall have that sort of extreme desire, that restless struggle, to throw off this burning world, then the time will have come for me to glimpse the Divine Truth.

Give up this little life of yours. What matters it if you die of starvation — you and I and thousands like us — so long as this nation lives? What matters it if this little life goes? Everyone has to die, the saint or the sinner, the rich or the poor. The body never remains for anyone. Arise and awake and be perfectly sincere. Give up your passive attitude, gird your loins and stand up.

The fact being that the Lord is in us, we are He, the eternal subject, the real ego, never to be objectified, and that all this objectifying process is mere waste of time and talent. When the soul becomes aware of this, it gives up objectifying and falls back more and more upon the subjective.

This is the evolution, less and less in the body and more and more in the mind — man the highest form, meaning in Sanskrit manas , thought — the animal that thinks and not the animal that "senses" only. This is what in theology is called "renunciation". The formation of society, the institution of marriage, the love for children, our good works, morality, and ethics are all different forms of renunciation.

All our lives in every society are the subjection of the will, the thirst, the desire. This surrender of the will or the fictitious self — or the desire to jump out of ourselves, as it were — the struggle still to objectify the subject — is the one phenomenon in this world of which all societies and social forms are various modes and stages. Love is the easiest and smoothest way towards the self-surrender or subjection of the will and hatred, the opposite.

Karma-Yoga is purifying the mind by means of work. Now if any work is done, good or bad, it must produce as a result a good or bad effect; no power can stay it, once the cause is present.

Therefore good action producing good Karma, and bad action, bad Karma, the soul will go on in eternal bondage without ever hoping for deliverance. Now Karma belongs only to the body or the mind, never to the Atman (Self); only it can cast a veil before the Atman.

The veil cast by bad Karma is ignorance. Good Karma has the power to strengthen the moral powers. And thus it creates non-attachment; it destroys the tendency towards bad Karma and thereby purifies the mind. But if the work is done with the intention of enjoyment, it then produces only that very enjoyment and does not purify the mind or Chitta.

Therefore all work should be done without any desire to enjoy the fruits thereof. All fear and all desire to enjoy here or hereafter must be banished for ever by the Karma-Yogi. Moreover, this Karma without desire of return will destroy the selfishness, which is the root of all bondage.

The watchword of the Karma-Yogi is "not I, but Thou", and no amount of self-sacrifice is too much for him. But he does this without any desire to go to heaven, or gain name or fame or any other benefit in this world.

Although the explanation and rationale of this unselfish work is only in Jnana-Yoga, yet the natural divinity of man makes him love all sacrifice simply for the good of others, without any ulterior motive, whatever his creed or opinion. Again, with many the bondage of wealth is very great; and Karma-Yoga is absolutely necessary for them as breaking the crystallisation that has gathered round their love of money.

He is free, he is great, who turns his back upon the world, who has renounced everything, who has controlled his passion, and who thirsts for peace. One may gain political and social independence, but if one is a slave to his passions and desires, one cannot feel the pure joy of real freedom.

It is in the nature of work to be impelled ordinarily by motive and by attachment. In the presence of an ever active Providence who notes even the sparrow's fall, how can man attach any importance to his own work? Will it not be a blasphemy to do so when we know that He is taking care of the minutest things in the world?

We have only to stand in awe and reverence before Him saying, "Thy will be done". The highest men cannot work, for in them there is no attachment. Those whose whole soul is gone into the Self, those whose desires are confined in the Self, who have become ever associated with the Self, for them there is no work.

Such are indeed the highest of mankind; but apart from them every one else has to work. In so working we should never think that we can help on even the least thing in this universe. We cannot. We only help ourselves in this gymnasium of the world. This is the proper attitude of work. If we work in this way, if we always remember that our present opportunity to work thus is a privilege which has been given to us, we shall never be attached to anything.

Millions like you and me think that we are great people in the world; but we all die, and in five minutes the world forgets us. But the life of God is infinite. "Who can live a moment, breathe a moment, if this all-powerful One does not will it?"

He is the ever active Providence. All power is His and within His command. Through His command the winds blow, the sun shines, the earth lives, and death stalks upon the earth. He is the all in all; He is all and in all. We can only worship Him.

Give up all fruits of work; do good for its own sake; then alone will come perfect non-attachment. The bonds of the heart will thus break, and we shall reap perfect freedom. This freedom is indeed the goal of Karma-Yoga.

Purification through Self-Denial

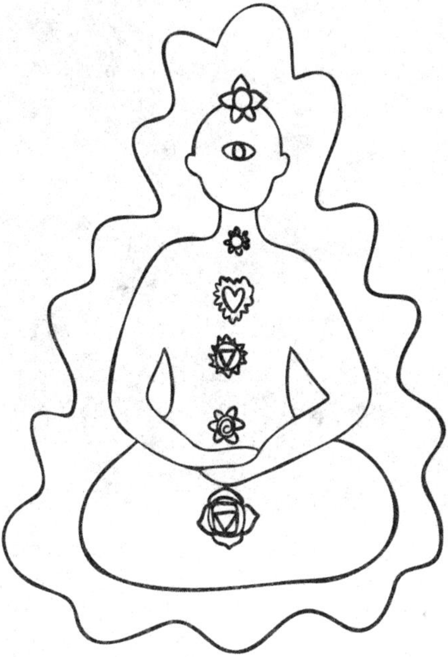

You will find various classes of men in this world. There are the God-men, whose self-abnegation is complete, and who do only good to others even at the sacrifice of their own lives. These are the highest of men. If there are a hundred of such in any country, that country need never despair.

But they are unfortunately too few. Then there are the good men who do good to others so long as it does not injure themselves. And there is a third class who, to do good to themselves, injure others.

It is said by a Sanskrit poet that there is a fourth unnamable class of people who injure others merely for injury's sake. Just as there are at one pole of existence the highest good men, who do good for the sake of doing good, so, at the other pole, there are others who injure others just for the sake of the injury. They do not gain anything thereby, but it is their nature to do evil.

Here are two Sanskrit words. The one is Pravritti, which means revolving towards, and the other is Nivritti, which means revolving away. The "revolving towards" is what we call the world, the "I and mine"; it includes all those things which are always enriching that "me" by wealth and money and power, and name and fame, and which are of a grasping nature, always tending to accumulate everything in one centre, that centre being "myself".

That is the Pravritti, the natural tendency of every human being; taking everything from everywhere and heaping it around one centre, that centre being man's own sweet self. When this tendency begins to break, when it is Nivritti or "going away from," then begin morality and religion. Both Pravritti and Nivritti are of the nature of work: the former is evil work, and the latter is good work.

This Nivritti is the fundamental basis of all morality and all religion, and the very perfection of it is entire self-abnegation, readiness to sacrifice mind and body and everything for another being. When a man has reached that state, he has attained to the perfection of Karma-Yoga.

It is not at all any question of creed, or doctrine — even men who are very much opposed to all religious ideas, when they see one of these acts of complete self-sacrifice, feel that they must revere it.

Have you not seen even a most bigoted Christian, when he reads Edwin Arnold's Light of Asia, stand in reverence of Buddha, who Preached no God, preached nothing but self-sacrifice?

The only thing is that the bigot does not know that his own end and aim in life is exactly the same as that of those from whom he differs. The worshipper, by keeping constantly before him the idea of God and a surrounding of good, comes to the same point at last and says, "Thy will be done," and keeps nothing to himself. That is self-abnegation.

The philosopher, with his knowledge, sees that the seeming self is a delusion and easily gives it up. It is self-abnegation. So Karma, Bhakti, and Jnana all meet here; and this is what was meant by all the great preachers of ancient times, when they taught that God is not the world.

There is one thing which is the world and another which is God; and this distinction is very true. What they mean by world is selfishness. Unselfishness is God. One may live on a throne, in a golden palace, and be perfectly unselfish; and then he is in God. Another may live in a hut and wear rags, and have nothing in the world; yet, if he is selfish, he is intensely merged in the world.

Every act of charity, every thought of sympathy, every action of help, every good deed, is taking so much of self-importance away from our little selves and making us think of ourselves as the lowest and the least, and, therefore, it is all good. Here we find that Jnana, Bhakti, and Karma — all come to one point.

The highest ideal is eternal and entire self-abnegation, where there is no "I," but all is "Thou"; and whether he is conscious or unconscious of it, Karma-Yoga leads man to that end. A religious preacher may become horrified at the idea of an Impersonal God; he may insist on a Personal God and wish to keep up his own identity and individuality, whatever he may mean by that.

But his ideas of ethics, if they are really good, cannot but be based on the highest self-abnegation. It is the basis of all morality; you may extend it to men, or animals, or angels, it is the one basic idea, the one fundamental principle running through all ethical systems.

The more a man throws himself away, the more God comes in, hence self abnegation, which is the secret of all religion and morality. Too many people bring down their ideals. They want a comfortable religion, but there is none such. It is all self-surrender and upward striving.

What is perfect self-abnegation? It means the abnegation of this apparent self, the abnegation of all selfishness. This idea of "me and mine" — Ahamkara and Mamata — is the result of past Superstition, and the more this present self passes away, the more the real Self becomes manifest.

This is true self-abnegation, the centre, the basis, the gist of all moral teaching; and whether man knows it or not the whole world is slowly going towards it, practicing it more or less. Only, the vast majority of mankind are doing it unconsciously. Let them do it consciously. Let then make the sacrifice, knowing that this "me and mine" is not the real Self, but only a limitation.

But one glimpse Of that infinite reality which is behind — but one spark of that infinite fire that is the All — represents the present man; the Infinite is his true nature.

If we are genuine Karma-Yogis and wish to train ourselves to that attainment of this state, wherever we may begin we are sure to end in perfect self-abnegation; and as soon as this seeming self has gone, the whole world, which at first appears to us to be filled with evil, will appear to be heaven itself and full of blessedness. Its very atmosphere will be blessed; every human face there will be god. Such is the end and aim of Karma-Yoga, and such is its perfection in practical life.

Infinite Patience

Are great things ever done smoothly? Time, patience, and indomitable will must show.

Every work has got to pass through hundreds of difficulties before succeeding. Those that persevere will see the light, sooner or later.

"Fortune favours the brave and energetic." Don't look back — forward, infinite energy, infinite enthusiasm, infinite daring, and infinite patience — then alone can great deeds be accomplished. We must set the whole world afire.

Have fire and spread all over. Work, work. Be the servant while leading, be unselfish, and never listen to one friend in private accusing another. Have infinite patience, and success is yours.

Have patience and be faithful unto death. Do not fight among yourselves. Be perfectly pure in money dealings… We will do great things yet… So long as you have faith and honesty and devotion, everything will prosper.

Shyness won't do any more.... He who has infinite patience and infinite energy at his back, will alone succeed.

Infinite patience, infinite purity, and infinite perseverance are the secret of success in a good cause.

The more heart you will be able to manifest, the greater will be the victory you achieve. It is only a few that understand the language of the brain, but everyone from the Creator down to a clump of grass, understands the language that comes from the heart.

But then, in our country, it is a case of rousing men that are, as it were, dead. It will take time, but if you have infinite patience and perseverance, success is bound to come. No mistake in that.

Know full well that patience is the best means of succeeds.

Know it for certain that without steady devotion for the Guru and unflinching patience and perseverance, nothing is to be achieved.

Love conquers in the long run. It won't do to become impatient — wait, wait — patience is bound to give success.

Can anything be done unless everybody exerts himself to his utmost? " " etc.— "It is the man of action, the lion-heart, that the Goddess of Wealth resorts to." No need for looking behind. FORWARD! We want infinite energy, infinite zeal, infinite courage, and infinite patience, then only will great things achieved.

Nothing else is necessary but these — love, sincerity, and patience.

Nothing shall be done in haste. Purity, patience, and perseverance are the three essentials to success and, above all, love. All time is yours, there is no indecent haste. Everything will come right if you are pure and sincere.

Persevere on, my brave lads, We have only just begun. Never despond! Never say enough!

Purity, perseverance, and energy— these three I want.

Purity, patience and perseverance overcome all obstacles. All great things must of necessity be slow.

The fruit falls from the tree when it gets ripe. So wait for the time to come. Do not hurry. Moreover, no one has the right to make others miserable by his foolish acts. Wait, have patience, everything will come right in time.

Those who really want to be Yogis must give up, once for all, this nibbling at things. Take up one idea. Make that one idea your life — think of it, dream of it, live on that idea. Let the brain, muscles, nerves, every part of your body, be full of that idea, and just leave every other idea alone.

This is the way to success, and this is the way great spiritual giants are produced. Others are mere talking machines. If we really want to be blessed, and make others blessed, we must go deeper.

The first step is not to disturb the mind, not to associate with persons whose ideas are disturbing. All of you know that certain persons, certain places, certain foods, repel you. Avoid them; and those who want to go to the highest, must avoid all company, good or bad.

Practise hard; whether you live or die does not matter. You have to plunge in and work, without thinking of the result. If you are brave enough, in six months you will be a perfect Yogi.

But those who take up just a bit of it and a little of everything else make no progress. It is of no use simply to take a course of lessons. To those who are full of Tamas, ignorant and dull — those whose minds never get fixed on any idea, who only crave for something to amuse them — religion and philosophy are simply objects of entertainment. These are the unpersevering. They hear a talk, think it very nice, and then go home and forget all about it.

To succeed, you must have tremendous perseverance, tremendous will. 'I will drink the ocean', says the persevering soul, 'at my will mountains will crumble up.' Have that sort of energy, that sort of will, work hard, and you will reach the goal.

Wait, my child, wait and work on. Patience, patience.

Rejoice that you have done so much. When you feel gloomy, think what has been done within the last year. How, rising from nothing, we have the eyes of the world fixed upon us now. Not only India, but the world outside, is expecting great things of us.

There was a great god-sage called Narada. Just as there are sages among mankind, great Yogis, so there are great Yogis among the gods. Narada was a good Yogi, and very great. He travelled everywhere.

One day he was passing through a forest, and saw a man who had been meditating until the white ants had built a huge mound round his body — so long had he been sitting in that position. He said to Narada, "Where are you going?"

Narada replied, "I am going to heaven."

"Then ask God when He will be merciful to me; when I shall attain freedom."

Further on Narada saw another man. He was jumping about, singing, dancing, and said, "Oh, Narada, where are you going?" His voice and his gestures were wild.

Narada said, "I am going to heaven."

"Then, ask when I shall be free."

Narada went on. In the course of time he came again by the same road, and there was the man who had been meditating with the ant-hill round him. He said, "Oh, Narada, did you ask the Lord about me?"

"Oh, yes."

"What did He say?"

"The Lord told me that you would attain freedom in four more births."

Then the man began to weep and wail, and said, "I have meditated until an ant-hill has grown around me, and I have four more births yet!"

Narada went to the other man. "Did you ask my question?"

"Oh, yes. Do you see this tamarind tree? I have to tell you that as many leaves as there are on that tree, so many times, you shall be born, and then you shall attain freedom."

The man began to dance for joy, and said, "I shall have freedom after such a short time!"

A voice came, "My child, you will have freedom this minute."

That was the reward for his perseverance. He was ready to work through all those births, nothing discouraged him. But the first man felt that even four more births were too long. Only perseverance, like that of the man who was willing to wait aeons brings about the highest result.

The most horrible thing about competition is that one may conquer the environments, but that where one may conquer, thousands are crowded out. So it is evil at best. That cannot be good which helps only one and hinders the majority. Patanjali says that these struggles remain only through our ignorance, and are not necessary, and are not part of the evolution of man. It is just our impatience which creates them.

We have not the patience to go and work our way out. For instance, there is a fire in a theatre, and only a few escape. The rest in trying to rush out crush one another down. That crush was not necessary for the salvation of the building nor of the two or three who escaped. If all had gone out slowly, not one would have been hurt.

That is the case in life. The doors are open for us, and we can all get out without the competition and struggle; and yet we struggle. The struggle we create through our own ignorance, through impatience; we are in too great a hurry. The highest manifestation of strength is to keep ourselves calm and on our own feet.

Attain Everything by Sacrifice

In the animal kingdom we really see such laws as struggle for existence, survival of the fittest, etc., evidently at work. Therefore Darwin's theory seems true to a certain extent. But in the human kingdom, where there is the manifestation of rationality, we find just the reverse of those laws.

For instance, in those whom we consider really great men or ideal characters, we scarcely observe any external struggle. In the animal kingdom instinct prevails; but the more a man advances, the more he manifests rationality.

For this reason, progress in the rational human kingdom cannot be achieved, like that in the animal kingdom, by the destruction of others! The highest evolution of man is effected through sacrifice alone. A man is great among his fellows in proportion as he can sacrifice for the sake of others, while in the lower strata of the animal kingdom, that animal is the strongest which can kill the greatest number of animals.

Hence the struggle theory is not equally applicable to both kingdoms. Man's struggle is in the mental sphere. A man is greater in proportion as he can control his mind. When the mind's activities are perfectly at rest, the Atman manifests Itself.

The struggle which we observe in the animal kingdom for the preservation of the gross body obtains in the human plane of existence for gaining mastery over the mind or for attaining the state of balance. Like a living tree and its reflection in the water of a tank, we find opposite kinds of struggle in the animal and human kingdoms.

Do all as a sacrifice or offering to the Lord. Be in the world, but not of it, like the lotus leaf whose roots are in the mud but which remains always pure. Let your love go to all, whatever they do to you.

A blind man cannot see colour, so how can we see evil unless it is in us? We compare what we see outside with what we find in ourselves and pronounce judgment accordingly. Do not want this world, because what you desire you get.

Seek the Lord and the Lord only. The more power there is, the more bondage, the more fear. How much more afraid and miserable are we than the ant! Get out of it all and come to the Lord. Seek the science of the maker and not that of the made.

Great things can be done by great sacrifices only. No selfishness, no name, no fame, yours or mine, nor my Master's even! Work, work the idea, the plan, my boys, my brave, noble, good souls — to the wheel, to the wheel put your shoulders!

Stop not to look back for name, or fame, or any such nonsense. Throw self overboard and work. Remember, "The grass when made into a rope by being joined together can even chain a mad elephant."

The Lord's blessings on you all! His power be in you all— as I believe it is already . "Wake up, stop not until the goal is reached", say the Vedas.

Where is that martial spirit which, at the very outset, requires one to know how to serve and obey and to practise self-restraint! The martial spirit is not self – assertion but self – sacrifice. One must be ready to advance and lay down one's life at the word of command, before he can command the hearts and lives of others. One must sacrifice himself first.

I know, and know for sure, that great things are done only by great sacrifices. I know for certain that India requires the sacrifice of her highest and best.

Throughout the history of the world you find great men make great sacrifices and the mass of mankind enjoy the benefit. If you want to give up everything for your own salvation, it is nothing. Do you want to forgo even your own salvation for the good of the world? You are God, think of that.

I want a band of young Bengal — who alone are the hope of this country. My hope of the future lies in the youths of character — intelligent, renouncing all for the service of others, and obedient — who can sacrifice their lives in working out my ideas and thereby do good to themselves and the country at large.

Otherwise, boys of the common run are coming in groups and will come. Dullness is written on their faces — their hearts are devoid of energy, their bodies feeble and unfit for work, and minds devoid of courage. What work will be done by these? If I get ten or twelve boys with the faith of Nachiketa, I can turn the thoughts and pursuits of this country in a new channel.

First, we have to understand the ideal, and then the methods by which we can make it practical. Those of you who are Sannyasins must try to do good to others, for Sannyasa means that.

There is no time to deliver a long discourse on "Renunciation", but I shall very briefly characterise it as "the love of death". Worldly people love life. The Sannyasin is to love death.

Are we to commit suicide then? Far from it. For suicides are not lovers of death, as it is often seen that when a man trying to commit suicide fails, he never attempts it for a second time.

What is the love of death then? We must die, that is certain; let us die then for a good cause. Let all our actions — eating, drinking, and everything that we do — tend towards the sacrifice of our self.

You nourish your body by eating. What good is there in doing that if you do not hold it as a sacrifice to the well-being of others? You nourish your minds by reading books. There is no good in doing that unless you hold it also as a sacrifice to the whole world. For the whole world is one; you are rated a very insignificant part of it, and therefore it is right for you that you should serve your millions of brothers rather than aggrandise this little self.

Thus you must die a gradual death. In such a death is heaven, all good is stored therein — and in its opposite is all that is diabolical and evil.

Then as to the methods of carrying the ideals into practical life. First, we have to understand that we must not have any impossible ideal. An ideal which is too high makes a nation weak and degraded. This happened after the Buddhistic and the Jain reforms.

On the other hand, too much practicality is also wrong. If you have not even a little imagination, if you have no ideal let guide you, you are simply a brute. So we must not lower our ideal, neither are we to lose sight of practicality. We must avoid the two extremes.

Let us be at peace, perfect peace, with ourselves, and give up our whole body and mind and everything as an eternal sacrifice unto the Lord. Instead of the sacrifice of pouring oblations into the fire, perform this one great sacrifice day and night — the sacrifice of your little self.

"In search of wealth in this world, Thou art the only wealth I have found; I sacrifice myself unto Thee. In search of some one to be loved, Thou art the only one beloved I have found; I sacrifice myself unto Thee."

Let us repeat this day and night, and say, “Nothing for me; no matter whether the thing is good, bad, or indifferent; I do not care for it; I sacrifice all unto Thee.”

Day and night let us renounce our seeming self until it becomes a habit with us to do so, until it gets into the blood, the nerves, and the brain, and the whole body is every moment obedient to this idea of self-renunciation. Go then into the midst of the battlefield, with the roaring cannon and the din of war, and you will find yourself to be free and at peace.

No great thing can be done without sacrifice. Who on seeing the tiny sprout of the banyan can imagine that in course of time it will develop into a gigantic banyan tree?The heart must be plucked out and the bleeding heart placed upon the altar.

Then great things are done. Is there any other way? None have found it. I appeal to each one of you, to those who have accomplished any great thing. Oh, how much it has cost! What agony! What torture! What terrible suffering is behind every deed of success in every life! You know that, all of you.

Nothing is gained except by sacrifice. he holiest function of our human consciousness, the noblest, do not make it unclean! Do not degrade it to the level of the brutes.... Make yourselves decent men! ... Be chaste and pure! ... There is no other way. Did Christ find any other way? ... If you can conserve and use the energy properly, it leads you to God. Inverted, it is hell itself.

One idea that I see clear as daylight is that misery is caused by ignorance and nothing else. Who will give the world light? Sacrifice in the past has been the Law, it will be, alas, for ages to come. The earth's bravest and best will have to sacrifice themselves for the good of many, for the welfare of all. Buddhas by the hundred are necessary with eternal love and pity.

Religions of the world have become lifeless mockeries. What the world wants is character. The world is in need of those whose life is one burning love, selfless. That love will make every word tell like thunderbolt.

Sacrifice of everything for the good of others is real Sannyasa. They have never enjoyed any good thing in life. See how simple they are. Can you mitigate their misery a little? Otherwise, of what good is the wearing of the Gerua robe?

No great work can be done without sacrifice. The Purusha Himself sacrificed Himself to create this world. Lay down your comforts, your pleasures, your names, fame or position, nay even your lives, and make a bridge of human chains over which millions will cross this ocean of life.

Bring all the forces of good together. Do not care under what banner you march. Do not care what be your colour — green, blue, or red — but mix up all the colours and produce that intense glow of white, the colour of love. Ours is to work. The results will take care of themselves.

If any social institution stands in your way of becoming God, it will give way before the power of Spirit. I do not see into the future; nor do I care to see. But one vision I see dear as life before me: that the ancient Mother has awakened once more, sitting on Her throne rejuvenated, more glorious than ever. Proclaim Her to all the world with the voice of peace and benediction.

Sacrifice on God's altar earth's purest and best. He who struggles is better than he who never attempts. Even to look on one who has given up has a purifying effect. Stand up for God; let the world go. Have no compromise.

Give up the world, then alone you are loosened from the body. When it dies, you are azad , free. Be free. Death alone can never free us. Freedom must be attained by our own efforts during life; then, when the body falls, there will be no rebirth for the free.

The two great watchwords of every great religion are renunciation and self – sacrifice. We all want the truth, and we know that it must come, whether we want it or not. In a way we are all striving for that good. And what prevents our reaching it? It is ourselves. Your ancestors used to call it the devil; but it is our own false self.

We live in slavery, and we would die if we were out of it. We are like the man who lived in total darkness for ninety years and when taken out into the warm sunshine of nature, prayed to be taken back to his dungeon. You would not leave this old life to go into a newer and greater freedom which opens out.

Sacrifice your life for the good of others and go round to the doors of people carrying this message of fearlessness — arise, awake, and stop not till the goal is reached.

"सन्निमित्ते वरं त्यागो विनाशे नियते सति—When death is certain, it is best to sacrifice oneself for a good cause."

We must plunge heart and soul and body into the work. Until we be ready to sacrifice everything else to one Idea and to one alone, we never, never will see the light. Those that want to help mankind must take their own pleasure and pain, name and fame, and all sorts of interests, and make a bundle of them and throw them into the sea, and then come to the Lord.

This is what all the Masters said and did. Was it ever in the history of the world that any great work was done by the rich? It is the heart and the brain that do it ever and ever and not the purse.

My idea and all my life with it — and to God for help; to none else! This is the only secret of success.

The ideal law may be that no man should covet the belongings of others, but the actual law is that a very large number do. Thus the word law used in regard to laws of nature has a very different interpretation when applied to ethics and human actions generally.

Analysing the ethical laws of the world and comparing them with the actual state of things, two laws stand out supreme. The one, that of repelling everything from us—separating ourselves from everyone—which leads to self-aggrandisement even at the cost of everyone else's happiness.

The other, that of self-sacrifice—of taking no thought of ourselves—only of others. Both spring from the search for happiness—one, of finding happiness in injuring others and the ability of feeling that happiness only in our own senses. The other, of finding happiness in doing good to others — the ability of feeling happy, as it were, through the senses of others.

The great and good of the world are those who have the latter power predominating. Yet both these are working side by side conjointly; in almost everyone they are found in mixture, one or the other predominating. The thief steals, perhaps, for someone he loves.

When you have men who are ready to sacrifice their everything for their country, sincere to the backbone — when such men arise, India will become great in every respect. It is the men that make the country!

What is there in the country? If you catch the social morality and the political morality of the Japanese, you will be as great as they are. The Japanese are ready to sacrifice everything for their country, and they have become a great people. But you are not; you cannot be, you sacrifice everything only for your own families and possessions.

⟵ ⟶

The Karma-Yogi wants everyone to be saved before himself. His only salvation is to help others to salvation. "To serve Krishna's servants is the highest worship." One great saint prayed, "Let me go to hell with the sins of the whole world, but let the world be saved." True worship leads to intense self – sacrifice.

⟵ ⟶

What good is it carrying along a load of bones and flesh! Initiated into the Mantra of extreme self-sacrifice for the sake of God, go, lay down for others this body of flesh and bones like the Muni Dadhichi! Those alone, say the Shastras, are the real Gurus, who have studied the Vedas and the Vedanta, who are knowers of the Brahman, who are able to lead others beyond to fearlessness; when such are at hand, get yourself initiated, "no speculation in such a case". Do you know what has become of this principle now? — "like the blind leading the blind"!

Love must conquer hatred, hatred cannot conquer itself. Materialism and all its miseries can never be conquered by materialism. Armies when they attempt to conquer armies only multiply and make brutes of humanity. Spirituality must conquer the West.

Where are the men ready to go out to every country in the world with the messages of the great sages of India? Where are the men who are ready to sacrifice everything, so that this message shall reach every corner of the world? Such heroic spurs are wanted to help the spread of truth.

Such heroic workers are wanted to go abroad and help to disseminate the great truths of the Vedanta. The world wants it; without it the world will be destroyed. The whole of the Western world is on a volcano which may burst tomorrow, go to pieces tomorrow. They have searched every corner of the world and have found no respite. They have drunk deep of the cup of pleasure and found it vanity. Now is the time to work so that India's spiritual ideas may penetrate deep into the West.

Therefore young men of Madras, I specially ask you to remember this. We must go out, we must conquer the world through our spirituality and philosophy. There is no other alternative, we must do it or die. The only condition of national life, of awakened and vigorous national life, is the conquest of the world by Indian thought.

As by continuing our religious practices we gradually develop a certain determined tendency for it, so by performing disinterested work over and over again, even unwillingly, we gradually find the will merging itself in it. The inclination to work for others develops in this way, do you see? Just do some such work even though unwillingly, and then see if the actual fruit of Tapasya is realised within or not. As the outcome of work for the sake of others, the angularities of the mind get smoothed down, and men are gradually prepared for sincere self-sacrifice for the good of others.

As the outcome of work for the sake of others, the angularities of the mind get smoothed down, and men are gradually prepared for sincere self – sacrifice for the good of others.

We should feel the Eternal Unity so much, that we should weep for all sinners, knowing that it is we who are sinning. The eternal law is self – sacrifice, not self – assertion. What self to assert when all is one? There are no "rights", all is love.

The great truths that Jesus taught have never been lived. Let us try his method and see if the world will not be saved. The contrary method has nearly destroyed it. Selflessness only, not selfishness, can solve the question.

The idea of "right" is a limitation; there is really no "mine" and "thine", for I am thou and thou art I. We have "responsibility", not "rights".

We should say, "I am the universe", not "I am John" or "I am Mary". These limitations are all delusions and are what holds us in bondage, for as soon as I think, "I am John", I want exclusive posses sion of certain things and begin to say "me and mine", and continually make new distinctions in so doing.

So our bondage goes on increasing with every fresh distinction, and we get further and further away from the central Unity, the undivided Infinite. There is only one Individual, and each of us is That.

Oneness alone is love and fearlessness; separation leads us to hatred and fear. Oneness fulfils the law. Here, on earth, we strive to enclose little spaces and exclude outsiders, but we cannot do that in the sky, though that is what sectarian religion tries to do when it says, "Only this way leads to salvation, all others are wrong".

Our aim should be to wipe out these little enclosures to widen the boundaries until they are lost sight of, and to realise that all religions lead to God. This little puny self must be sacrificed. This is the truth symbolised by baptism into a new life, the death of the old man, the birth of the new — the perishing of the false self, the realisation of the Atman, the one Self of the universe.

It is more blessed, in my opinion, even to go wrong, impelled by one's free will and intelligence than to be good as an automaton. Again, can that be called society which is formed by an aggregate of men who are like lumps of clay, like lifeless machines, like heaped up pebbles?

How can such society fare well? Were good possible, then instead of being slaves for hundreds of years, we would have been the greatest nation on earth, and this soil of India, instead of being a mine of stupidity, would have been the eternal fountain-head of learning. Is not self-sacrifice, then, a virtue? Is it not the most virtuous deed to sacrifice the happiness of one, the welfare of one, for the sake of the many?

It is all a degeneration which has its root in selfishness. That in boarding a steamer one follows the vulgar maxim, "Uncle, save thy own precious skin", and in music and moments of recreation everyone tries to make a display of himself, is a typical picture of our mental state. Only a little training in self – sacrifice would take it away. It is the fault of the parents who do not teach their children good manners. Self – sacrifice, indeed, is the basis of all civilization.

Exactly, but as the Bengali adage goes, "Can beauty be manufactured by rubbing and scrubbing? Can love be generated by effort and compulsion?" What glory is there in the renunciation of an eternal beggar? What virtue is there in the sense- control of one devoid of sense-power?

What again is the self-sacrifice of one devoid of idea, devoid of heart, devoid of high ambition, and devoid of the conception of what constitutes society? What expression of devotedness to a husband is there by forcing a widow to commit Sati? Why make people do virtuous deeds by teaching superstitions?

I say, liberate, undo the shackles of people as much as you can. Can dirt be washed by dirt? Can bondage be removed by bondage? Where is the instance? When you would be able to sacrifice all desire for happiness for the sake of society, then you would be the Buddha, then you would be free: that is far off.

Again, do you think the way to do it lies through oppression? "Oh, what examples or self-denial are our widows! Oh, how sweet is child-marriage! Is another such custom possible! Can there be anything but love between husband and wife in such a marriage!" such is the whine going round nowadays.

But as to the men, the masters of the situation, there is no need of self-denial for them! Is there a virtue higher than serving others? But the same does not apply to Brahmins — you others do it!

The truth is that in this country parents and relatives can ruthlessly sacrifice the best interests of their children and others for their own selfish ends to save themselves by compromise to society; and the teaching of generations rendering the mind callous has made it perfectly easy. He, the brave alone, can deny self. The coward, afraid of the lash, with one hand wipes his eyes and gives with the other.

Of what avail are such gifts? It is a far cry to love universal. The young plant should be hedged in and taken care of. One can hope gradually to attain to universal love if one can learn to love one object unselfishly. If devotion to one particular Ishta-Deva is attained, devotion to the universal Virat is gradually possible.

Therefore, when one has been able to deny self for an individual, one should talk of self-sacrifice for the sake of society, not before. It is action with desire that leads to action without desire. Is the renunciation of desire possible if desire did not exist in the beginning? And what could it mean? Can light have any meaning if there is no darkness?

Worship with desire, with attachment, comes first. Commence with the worship of the little, then the greater will come of itself.

The Powerful Maya

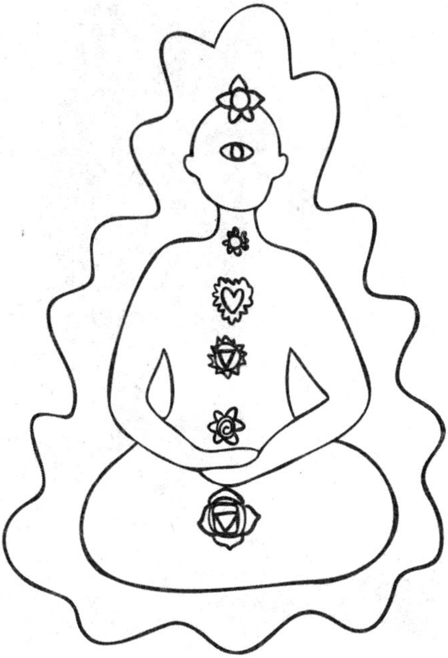

The theory of Maya forms one of the pillars upon which the Vedanta rests; it is, therefore, necessary that it should be properly understood. I ask a little patience of you, for there is a great danger of its being misunderstood.

The oldest idea of Maya that we find in Vedic literature is the sense of delusion; but then the real theory had not been reached. We find such passages as, "Indra through his Maya assumed various forms." Here it is true the word Maya means something like magic, and we find various other passages, always taking the same meaning. The word Maya then dropped out of sight altogether.

But in the meantime the idea was developing. Later, the question was raised: "Why can't we know this secret of the universe?" And the answer given was very significant: "Because we talk in vain, and because we are satisfied with the things of the senses, and because we are running after desires; therefore, we, as it were, cover the Reality with a mist."

Here the word Maya is not used at all, but we get the idea that the cause of our ignorance is a kind of mist that has come between us and the Truth. Much later on, in one of the latest Upanishads, we find the word Maya reappearing, but this time, a transformation has taken place in it, and a mass of new meaning has attached itself to the word.

Theories had been propounded and repeated, others had been taken up, until at last the idea of Maya became fixed. We read in the Shvetashvatara Upanishad, "Know nature to be Maya and the Ruler of this Maya is the Lord Himself."

Coming to our philosophers, we find that this word Maya has been manipulated in various fashions, until we come to the great Shankaracharya. The theory of Maya was manipulated a little by the Buddhists too, but in the hands of the Buddhists it became very much like what is called Idealism, and that is the meaning that is now generally given to the word Maya.

When the Hindu says the world is Maya, at once people get the idea that the world is an illusion. This interpretation has some basis, as coming through the Buddhistic philosophers, because there was one section of philosophers who did not believe in the external world at all. But the Maya of the Vedanta, in its last developed form, is neither Idealism nor Realism, nor is it a theory. It is a simple statement of facts — what we are and what we see around us.

The theory of Maya is as old as the Rik-Samhita. The Shvetashvatara Upanishad contains the word "Maya" which is developed out of Prakriti.

A legend tells how once Narada said to Krishna, "Lord, show me Maya." A few days passed away, and Krishna asked Narada to make a trip with him towards a desert, and after walking for several miles, Krishna said, "Narada, I am thirsty; can you fetch some water for me?" "I will go at once, sir, and get you water."

So Narada went. At a little distance there was a village; he entered the village in search of water and knocked at a door, which was opened by a most beautiful young girl. At the sight of her he immediately forgot that his Master was waiting for water, perhaps dying for the want of it. He forgot everything and began to talk with the girl. All that day he did not return to his Master.

The next day, he was again at the house, talking to the girl. That talk ripened into love; he asked the father for the daughter, and they were married and lived there and had children.

Thus twelve years passed. His father-in-law died, he inherited his property. He lived, as he seemed to think, a very happy life with his wife and children, his fields and his cattle and so forth.

Then came a flood. One night the river rose until it overflowed its banks and flooded the whole village. Houses fell, men and animals were swept away and drowned, and everything was floating in the rush of the stream. Narada had to escape. With one hand be held his wife, and with the other two of his children; another child was on his shoulders, and he was trying to ford this tremendous flood.

After a few steps he found the current was too strong, and the child on his shoulders fell and was borne away. A cry of despair came from Narada. In trying to save that child, he lost his grasp upon one of the others, and it also was lost. At last his wife, whom he clasped with all his might, was torn away by the current, and he was thrown on the bank, weeping and wailing in bitter lamentation.

Behind him there came a gentle voice, "My child, where is the water? You went to fetch a pitcher of water, and I am waiting for you; you have been gone for quite half an hour." "Half an hour! " Narada exclaimed. Twelve whole years had passed through his mind, and all these scenes had happened in half an hour! And this is Maya.

Reformers arise and preach that learning, wealth, and culture should not be in the hands of a select few; and they do their best to make them accessible to all. These may bring more happiness to some, but, perhaps, as culture comes, physical happiness lessens. The knowledge of happiness brings the knowledge of unhappiness.

Which way then shall we go? The least amount of material prosperity that we enjoy is causing the same amount of misery elsewhere. This is the law. The young, perhaps, do not see it clearly, but those who have lived long enough and those who have struggled enough will understand it. And this is Maya.

These things are going on, day and night, and to find a solution of this problem is impossible. Why should it be so? It is impossible to answer this, because the question cannot be logically formulated. There is neither how nor why in fact; we only know that it is and that we cannot help it. Even to grasp it, to draw an exact image of it in our own mind, is beyond our power. How can we solve it then?

Maya is a statement of the fact of this universe, of how it is going on. People generally get frightened when these things are told to them. But bold we must be. Hiding facts is not the way to find a remedy.

As you all know, a hare hunted by dogs puts its head down and thinks itself safe; so, when we run into optimism; we do just like the hare, but that is no remedy. There are objections against this, but you may remark that they are generally from people who possess many of the good things of life. In this country (England) it is very difficult to become a pessimist.

Everyone tells me how wonderfully the world is going on, how progressive; but what he himself is, is his own world. Old questions arise: Christianity must be the only true religion of the world because Christian nations are prosperous! But that assertion contradicts itself, because the prosperity of the Christian nation depends on the misfortune of non-Christian nations. There must be some to prey on.

Suppose the whole world were to become Christian, then the Christian nations would become poor, because there would be no non-Christian nations for them to prey upon. Thus the argument kills itself. Animals are living upon plants, men upon animals and, worst of all, upon one another, the strong upon the weak. This is going on everywhere. And this is Maya.

What solution do you find for this? We hear every day many explanations, and are told that in the long run all will be good. Taking it for granted that this is possible, why should there be this diabolical way of doing good?

Why cannot good be done through good, instead of through these diabolical methods? The descendants of the human beings of today will be happy; but why must there be all this suffering now? There is no solution. This is Maya.

Again, we often hear that it is one of the features of evolution that it eliminates evil, and this evil being continually eliminated from the world, at last only good will remain. That is very nice to hear, and it panders to the vanity of those who have enough of this world's goods, who have not a hard struggle to face every day and are not being crushed under the wheel of this so-called evolution. It is very good and comforting indeed to such fortunate ones. The common herd may surfer, but they do not care; let them die, they are of no consequence.

Very good, yet this argument is fallacious from beginning to end. It takes for granted, in the first place, that manifested good and evil in this world are two absolute realities. In the second place, it makes a still worse assumption that the amount of good is an increasing quantity and the amount of evil is a decreasing quantity.

So, if evil is being eliminated in this way by what they call evolution, there will come a time when all this evil will be eliminated and what remains will be all good. Very easy to say, but can it be proved that evil is a lessening quantity?

Take, for instance, the man who lives in a forest, who does not know how to cultivate the mind, cannot read a book, has not heard of such a thing as writing. If he is severely wounded, he is soon all right again; while we die if we get a scratch. Machines are making things cheap, making for progress and evolution, but millions are crushed, that one may become rich; while one becomes rich, thousands at the same time become poorer and poorer, and whole masses of human beings are made slaves.

That way it is going on. The animal man lives in the senses. If he does not get enough to eat, he is miserable; or if something happens to his body, he is miserable. In the senses both his misery and his happiness begin and end. As soon as this man progresses, as soon as his horizon of happiness increases, his horizon of unhappiness increases proportionately.

The man in the forest does not know what it is to be jealous, to be in the law courts, to pay taxes, to be blamed by society, to be ruled over day and night by the most tremendous tyranny that human diabolism ever invented, which pries into the secrets of every human heart. He does not know how man becomes a thousand times more diabolical than any other animal, with all his vain knowledge and with all his pride.

Thus it is that, as we emerge out of the senses, we develop higher powers of enjoyment, and at the same time we have to develop higher powers of suffering too. The nerves become finer and capable off more suffering. In every society, we often find that the ignorant, common man, when abused, does not feel much, but he feels a good thrashing.

But the gentleman cannot bear a single word of abuse; he has become so finely nerved. Misery has increased with his susceptibility to happiness. This does not go much to prove the evolutionist's case.

As we increase our power to be happy, we also increase our power to suffer, and sometimes I am inclined to think that if we increase our power to become happy in arithmetical progression, we shall increase, on the other hand, our power to become miserable in geometrical progression. We who are progressing know that the more we progress, the more avenues are opened to pain as well as to pleasure. And this is Maya.

Thus we find that Maya is not a theory for the explanation of the world; it is simply a statement of facts as they exist, that the very basis of our being is contradiction, that everywhere we have to move through this tremendous contradiction, that wherever there is good, there must also be evil, and wherever there is evil, there must be some good, wherever there is life, death must follow as its shadow, and everyone who smiles will have to weep, and vice versa.

Nor can this state of things be remedied. We may verily imagine that there will be a place where there will be only good and no evil, where we shall only smile and never weep. This is impossible in the very nature of things; for the conditions will remain the same. Wherever there is the power of producing a smile in us, there lurks the power of producing tears. Wherever there is the power of producing happiness, there lurks somewhere the power of making us miserable.

As long as we recognise duality, or separate God and man, so long we must see good and evil. Only by going to the centre, by unifying ourselves with God can we escape the delusions of the senses.

When we let go the eternal fever of desire, the endless thirst that gives us no rest, when we have for ever quenched desire, we shall escape both good and evil, because we shall have transcended both. The satisfaction of desire only increases it, as oil poured on fire but makes it burn more fiercely.

The further from the centre, the faster goes the wheel, the less the rest. Draw near the centre, check desire, stamp it out, let the false self go, then our vision will clear and we shall see God.

Only through renunciation of this life and of all life to come (heaven etc.), can we reach the point where we stand firmly on the true Self. While we hope for anything, desire still rules us. Be for one moment really "hopeless", and the mist will clear.

For what to hope when one is the all of existence? The secret of Jnana is to give up all and be sufficient unto ourselves. Say "not", and you become "not"; say "is", and you become "is". Worship the Self within, naught else exists. All that binds us is Maya-delusion.

When one is in ignorance, he sees the phenomenon and does not see God. When he sees God, this universe vanishes entirely for him. Ignorance or Maya, as it is called, is the cause of all this phenomenon — the Absolute, the Unchangeable, being taken as this manifested universe.

This Maya is not absolute zero, nor non-existence. It is defined as neither existence nor non-existence. It is not existence, because that can be said only of the Absolute, the Unchangeable, and in this sense, Maya is non-existence.

Again, it cannot be said it is non-existence; for if it were, it could never produce phenomenon. So it is something which is neither; and in the Vedanta philosophy it is called Anirvachaniya or inexpressible.

Maya, then, is the real cause of this universe. Maya gives the name and form to what Brahman or God gives the material; and the latter seems to have been transformed into all this.

The Advaitists, then, have no place for the individual soul. They say individual souls are created by Maya. In reality they cannot exist. If there were only one existence throughout, how could it be that I am one, and you are one, and so forth?

We are all one, and the cause of evil is the perception of duality. As soon as I begin to feel that I am separate from this universe, then first comes fear, and then comes misery. "Where one hears another, one sees another, that is small. Where one does not see another, where one does not hear another, that is the greatest, that is God. In that greatest is perfect happiness. In small things there is no happiness."

Everyone is as much bound in thought, word, deed, and mind, as a piece of stone or this table. That I talk to you now is as rigorous in causation as that you listen to me. There is no freedom until you go beyond Maya. That is the real freedom of the soul. Men, however sharp and intellectual, however clearly they see the force of the logic that nothing here can be free, are all compelled to think they are free; they cannot help it.

No work can go on until we begin to say we are free. It means that the freedom we talk about is the glimpse of the blue sky through the clouds and that the real freedom — the blue sky itself — is behind.

True freedom cannot exist in the midst of this delusion, this hallucination, this nonsense of the world, this universe of the senses, body, and mind. All these dreams, without beginning or end, uncontrolled and uncontrollable, ill-adjusted, broken, inharmonious, form our idea of this universe.

In a dream, when you see a giant with twenty heads chasing you, and you are flying from him, you do not think it is inharmonious; you think it is proper and right. So is this law. All that you call law is simply chance without meaning. In this dream state you call it law.

Within Maya, so far as this law of time, space and causation exists, there is no freedom; and all these various forms of worship are within this Maya. The idea of God and the ideas of brute and of man are within this Maya, and as such are equally hallucinations; all of them are dreams.

But you must take care not to argue like some extraordinary men of whom we hear at the present time. They say the idea of God is a delusion, but the idea of this world is true. Both ideas stand or fall by the same logic. He alone has the right to be an atheist who denies this world, as well as the other.

The same argument is for both. The same mass of delusion extends from God to the lowest animal, from a blade of grass to the Creator. They stand or fall by the same logic. The same person who sees falsity in the idea of God ought also to see it in the idea of his own body or his own mind.

When God vanishes, then also vanish the body and mind; and when both vanish, that which is the Real Existence remains for ever. "There the eyes cannot go, nor the speech, nor the mind. We cannot see it, neither know it."

And we now understand that so far as speech and thought and knowledge and intellect go, it is all within this Maya within bondage. Beyond that is Reality. There neither thought, nor mind, nor speech, can reach.

So far it is intellectually all right, but then comes the practice. The real work is in the practice.

Are any practices necessary to realise this Oneness? Most decidedly. It is not that you become this Brahman. You are already that. It is not that you are going to become God or perfect; you are already perfect; and whenever you think you are not, it is a delusion. This delusion which says that you are Mr. So-and-so or Mrs. So-and-so can be got rid of by another delusion, and that is practice.

Fire will eat fire, and you can use one delusion to conquer another delusion. One cloud will come and brush away another cloud, and then both will go away.

What are these practices then? We must always bear in mind that we are not going to be free, but are free already. Every idea that we are bound is a delusion. Every idea that we are happy or unhappy is a tremendous delusion; and another delusion will come — that we have got to work and worship and struggle to be free — and this will chase out the first delusion, and then both will stop.

To injure another creates bondage and hides the truth. Negative virtues are not enough; we have to conquer Maya, and then she will follow us. We only deserve things when they cease to bind us. When the bondage ceases, really and truly, all things come to us. Only those who want nothing are masters of nature.

The animal man lives in the senses. If he does not get enough to eat, he is miserable; or if something happens to his body, he is miserable. In the senses both his misery and his happiness begin and end. As soon as this man progresses, as soon as his horizon of happiness increases, his horizon of unhappiness increases proportionately.

The man in the forest does not know what it is to be jealous, to be in the law courts, to pay taxes, to be blamed by society, to be ruled over day and night by the most tremendous tyranny that human diabolism ever invented, which pries into the secrets of every human heart. He does not know how man becomes a thousand times more diabolical than any other animal, with all his vain knowledge and with all his pride.

Thus it is that, as we emerge out of the senses, we develop higher powers of enjoyment, and at the same time we have to develop higher powers of suffering too. The nerves become finer and capable off more suffering. In every society, we often find that the ignorant, common man, when abused, does not feel much, but he feels a good thrashing.

But the gentleman cannot bear a single word of abuse; he has become so finely nerved. Misery has increased with his susceptibility to happiness. This does not go much to prove the evolutionist's case.

As we increase our power to be happy, we also increase our power to suffer, and sometimes I am inclined to think that if we increase our power to become happy in arithmetical progression, we shall increase, on the other hand, our power to become miserable in geometrical progression. We who are progressing know that the more we progress, the more avenues are opened to pain as well as to pleasure. And this is Maya.

Thus we find that Maya is not a theory for the explanation of the world; it is simply a statement of facts as they exist, that the very basis of our being is contradiction, that everywhere we have to move through this tremendous contradiction, that wherever there is good, there must also be evil, and wherever there is evil, there must be some good, wherever there is life, death must follow as its shadow, and everyone who smiles will have to weep, and vice versa.

Nor can this state of things be remedied. We may verily imagine that there will be a place where there will be only good and no evil, where we shall only smile and never weep. This is impossible in the very nature of things; for the conditions will remain the same. Wherever there is the power of producing a smile in us, there lurks the power of producing tears. Wherever there is the power of producing happiness, there lurks somewhere the power of making us miserable.

Cause and effect are all Maya, and we shall grow to understand that all we see is as disconnected as the child's fairy tales now seem to us. There is really no such thing as cause and effect and we shall come to know it.

Then if you can, lower your intellect to let any allegory pass through your mind without questioning about connection. Develop love of imagery and beautiful poetry and then enjoy all mythologies as poetry.

Come not to mythology with ideas of history and reasoning. Let it flow as a current through your mind, let it be whirled as a candle before your eyes, without asking who holds the candle, and you will get the circle; the residuum of truth will remain in your mind.

Consciousness is a bondage. The argument from design claims that intelligence precedes form; but if intelligence is the cause of anything, it itself is in its turn an effect. It is Maya. God creates us, and we create God, and this is Maya.

The circle is unbroken; mind creates body, and body creates mind; the egg brings the chicken, the chicken the egg; the tree the seed, the seed the tree. The world is neither entirely differentiated nor yet entirely homogeneous. Man is free and must rise above both sides. Both are right in their place; but to reach truth, "isness", we must transcend all that we now know of existence, will, consciousness, doing, going, knowing.

There is no real individuality of the Jiva (separate soul); eventually it, as a compound, will go to pieces. Only that which is beyond further analysis is "simple", and that alone is truth, freedom, immortality, bliss.

All struggles for the preservation of this illusive individuality are really vices. All struggles to lose this individuality are virtues. Everything in the universe is trying to break down this individuality, either consciously or unconsciously. All morality is based upon the destruction of separateness or false individuality, because that is the cause of all sin.

Morality exists first; later, religion codifies it. Customs come first, and then mythology follows to explain them. While things are happening, they come by a higher law than reasoning; that arises later in the attempt to understand them. Reasoning is not the motive power, it is "chewing the cud" afterwards. Reason is the historian of the actions of the human beings.

In this world of Maya one need not injure, but "spread the hood, without striking". That is enough.

Delusion creates delusion. Delusion creates itself and destroys itself, such is Maya. All knowledge (so-called), being based on Maya, is a vicious circle, and in time that very knowledge destroys itself. "Let go the rope", delusion cannot touch the Atman. When we lay hold of the rope — identify ourselves with Maya — she has power over us. Let go of it, be the Witness only, then you can admire the picture of the universe undisturbed.

Maya is not illusion as it is popularly interpreted. Maya is real, yet it is not real. It is real in that the Real is behind it and gives it its appearance of reality. That which is real in Maya is the Reality in and through Maya. Yet the Reality is never seen ; and hence that which is seen is unreal, and it has no real independent existence of itself, but is dependent upon the Real for its existence.

Maya then is a paradox—real, yet not real, an illusion, yet not an illusion. He who knows the Real sees in Maya not illusion, but reality. He who knows not the Real sees in Maya illusion and thinks it real.

What we call nature is not the substance, unchanging and indestructible. Nature is time, space and causation. Nature is name and form. Nature is Maya. Maya means name and form, into which everything is cast. Maya is not real. We could not destroy it or change it if it were real. The substance is the noumenon, Maya is phenomena. There is the real "me" which nothing can destroy, and there is the phenomenal "me" which is continually changing and disappearing.

Advaita means non-duality; there are no two, but one. Yet we see that here is a proposition that the Absolute is manifesting Itself as many, through the veil of time, space, and causation. Therefore it seems that here are two, the Absolute and Maya (the sum total of time, space, and causation).

It seems apparently very convincing that there are two. To this the Advaitist replies that it cannot be called two. To have two, we must have two absolute independent existences which cannot be caused.

In the first place time, space, and causation cannot be said to be independent existences. Time is entirely a dependent existence; it changes with every change of our mind. Sometimes in dream one imagines that one has lived several years, at other times several months were passed as one second. So, time is entirely dependent on our state of mind.

Secondly, the idea of time vanishes altogether, sometimes. So with space. We cannot know what space is. Yet it is there, indefinable, and cannot exist separate from anything else. So with causation.

The one peculiar attribute we find in time, space, and causation is that they cannot exist separate from other things. Try to think of space without colour, or limits, or any connection with the things around — just abstract space. You cannot; you have to think of it as the space between two limits or between three objects. It has to be connected with some object to have any existence.

So with time; you cannot have any idea of abstract time, but you have to take two events, one preceding and the other succeeding, and join the two events by the idea of succession. Time depends on two events, just as space has to be related to outside objects. And the idea of causation is inseparable from time and space.

This is the peculiar thing about them that they have no independent existence. They have not even the existence which the chair or the wall has. They are as shadows around everything which you cannot catch. They have no real existence; yet they are not non-existent, seeing that through them all things are manifesting as this universe.

Thus we see, first, that the combination of time, space, and causation has neither existence nor non-existence. Secondly, it sometimes vanishes. To give an illustration, there is a wave on the ocean. The wave is the same as the ocean certainly, and yet we know it is a wave, and as such different from the ocean.

What makes this difference? The name and the form, that is, the idea in the mind and the form. Now, can we think of a wave-form as something separate from the ocean? Certainly not. It is always associated with the ocean idea. If the wave subsides, the form vanishes in a moment, and yet the form was not a delusion. So long as the wave existed the form was there, and you were bound to see the form. This is Maya.

What you call matter, or spirit, or mind, or anything else you may like to call them, the fact remains the same: we cannot say that they are, we cannot say that they are not. We cannot say they are one, we cannot say they are many. This eternal play of light and darkness — indiscriminate, indistinguishable, inseparable — is always there.

A fact, yet at the same time not a fact; awake and at the same time asleep. This is a statement of facts, and this is what is called Maya. We are born in this Maya, we live in it, we think in it, we dream in it. We are philosophers in it, we are spiritual men in it, nay, we are devils in this Maya, and we are gods in this Maya.

Stretch your ideas as far as you can make them higher and higher, call them infinite or by any other name you please, even these ideas are within this Maya. It cannot be otherwise, and the whole of human knowledge is a generalization of this Maya trying to know it as it appears to be.

This is the work of Nama-Rupa — name and form. Everything that has form, everything that calls up an idea in your mind, is within Maya; for everything that is bound by the laws of time, space, and causation is within Maya.

In the scriptures on Bhakti, five different paths of relationship are mentioned, by any of which one can attain to God; but another one can very well be added to them, viz. the path of meditation on the non-separateness, or oneness with God.

Thus the Bhakta can call the Advaitins Bhaktas as well, but of the non-differentiating type. As long as one is within the region of Maya, so long the idea of duality will no doubt remain. Space-time-causation, or name-and-form, is what is called Maya. When one goes beyond this Maya, then only the Oneness is realised, and then man is neither a dualist nor an Advaitist — to him all is One.

There is one thing between the metaphysical and the moral aspect of Advaitism; it is the theory of Maya. Everyone of these points in the Advaita system requires years to understand and months to explain.

Therefore you will excuse me if I only just touch them en passant. This theory of Maya has been the most difficult thing to understand in all ages. Let me tell you in a few words that it is surely no theory, it is the combination of the three ideas Desha-Kala-Nimitta — space, time, and causation — and this time and space and cause have been further reduced into Nama-Rupa. Suppose there is a wave in the ocean.

The wave is distinct from the ocean only in its form and name, and this form and this name cannot have any separate existence from the wave; they exist only with the wave. The wave may subside, but the same amount of water remains, even if the name and form that were on the wave vanish for ever.

So this Maya is what makes the difference between me and you, between all animals and man, between gods and men. In fact, it is this Maya that causes the Atman to be caught, as it were, in so many millions of beings, and these are distinguishable only through name and form. If you leave it alone, let name and form go, all this variety vanishes for ever, and you are what you really are. This is Maya.

We sometimes indicate a thing by describing its surroundings. When we say "Sachchidananda" (Existence-Knowledge-Bliss), we are merely indicating the shores of an indescribable Beyond. Not even can we say "is" about it, for that too is relative. Any imagination, any concept is in vain. Neti, neti ("Not this, not this") is all that can be said, for even to think is to limit and so to lose.

The senses cheat you day and night. Vedanta found that out ages ago; modern science is just discovering the same fact. A picture has only length and breadth, and the painter copies nature in her cheating by artificially giving the appearance of depth. No two people see the same world.

The highest knowledge will show you that there is no motion, no change in anything; that the very idea of it is all Maya. Study nature as a whole, that is, study motion. Mind and body are not our real self; both belong to nature, but eventually we can know the ding an sich. Then mind and body being transcended, all that they conceive goes. When you cease utterly to know and see the world, then you realise Atman. The superseding of relative knowledge is what we want. There is no infinite mind or infinite knowledge, because both mind and knowledge are limited.

We are now seeing through a veil; then we reach the "x", which is the Reality of all our knowing. If we look at a picture through a pin-hole in a cardboard, we get an utterly mistaken notion; yet what we see is really the picture. As we enlarge the hole, we get a clearer and clearer idea.

Out of the reality we manufacture the different views in conformity with our mistaken perceptions of name and form. When we throw away the cardboard, we see the same picture, but we see it as it is. We put in all the attributes, all the errors; the picture itself is unaltered thereby.

That is because Atman is the reality of all; all we see is Atman, but not as we see it, as name and form; they are all in our veil, in Maya.

They are like spots in the object-glass of a telescope, yet it is the light of the sun that shows us the spots; we could not even see the illusion save for the background of reality which is Brahman. Swami Vivekananda is just the speck on the object-glass; I am Atman, real, unchangeable, and that reality alone enables me to see Swami Vivekananda.

Atman is the essence of every hallucination; but the sun is never identified with the spots on the glass, it only shows them to us. Our actions, as they are evil or good, increase or decrease the "spots"; but they never affect the God within us. Perfectly cleanse the mind of spots and instantly we see, "I and my father are one".

We first perceive, then reason later. We must have this perception as a fact, and it is called religion, realisation. No matter if one never heard of creed or prophet or book. Let him get this realisation, and he needs no more. Cleanse the mind, this is all of religion; and until we ourselves clear off the spots, we cannot see the Reality as it is.

The baby sees no sun; he has not yet the measure of it in himself. Get rid of the defects within yourself, and you will not be able to see any without.

A baby sees robbery done, and it means nothing to him. Once you find the hidden object in a puzzle picture, you see it ever more; so when once you are free and stainless, you see only freedom and purity in the world around. That moment all the knots of the heart are cut asunder, all crooked places are made straight, and this world vanishes as a dream. And when we awake, we wonder how we ever came to dream such trash!

According to the Advaita philosophy, there is only one thing real in the universe, which it calls Brahman; everything else is unreal, manifested and manufactured out of Brahman by the power of Maya. To reach back to that Brahman is our goal.

We are, each one of us, that Brahman, that Reality, plus this Maya. If we can get rid of this Maya or ignorance, then we become what we really are. According to this philosophy, each man consists of three parts — the body, the internal organ or the mind, and behind that, what is called the Atman, the Self.

The body is the external coating and the mind is the internal coating of the Atman who is the real perceiver, the real enjoyer, the being in the body who is working the body by means of the internal organ or the mind.

"Om tat sat" is the only thing beyond Maya, but God exists eternally. As long as the Niagara Falls exist, the rainbow will exist; but the water continually flows away. The falls are the universe, and the rainbow is personal God; and both are eternal. While the universe exists, God must exist.

God creates the universe, and the universe creates God; and both are eternal. Maya is neither existence nor non-existence. Both the Niagara Falls and the rainbow are eternally changeable. . . . Brahman seen through Maya. Persians and Christians split Maya into two and call the good half "God" and the bad half the "devil". Vedanta takes Maya as a whole and recognises a unity beyond it — Brahman. . .

The mission of the Institute of Thought and Philosophy is to preserve and propagate the teachings of Swami Vivekananda. This great Indian spiritual leader is known for introducing the West to Hinduism. Drawing from his vast literary legacy, we provide valuable insights and practical guidance for modern living.

Have any query or feedback? Please reach out to us at ITPPress123@gmail.com